Christmas Stories And Legends

COMPILED BY

PHEBE A. CURTISS

Author of "White Gifts for the King"

Various

[ZHINGOORA BOOKS]

CONTENTS

THE LEGEND OF THE "WHITE GIFTS"

As Told by Phebe A. Curtiss

A great many years ago in a land far away from us there was a certain king who was dearly beloved by all of his people. Men admired him because he was strong and just. In all of his dealings they knew they could depend upon him. Every matter that came to his consideration was carefully weighed in his mind and his decisions were always wise. Women trusted him because he was pure and true, with lofty thoughts and high ambitions, and the children loved him because of his gentleness and tenderness toward them. He was never so burdened with affairs of state that he could not stop to speak a pleasant word of greeting to the tiniest child, and the very poorest of his subjects knew they could count upon his interest in them.

This deep-seated love and reverence for their king made the people of this country wish very much for a way in which to give expression to it so that he would understand it. Many consultations were held and one after another the plans suggested were rejected, but at last a most happy solution was found. It was rapidly circulated here and there and it met with the most hearty approval everywhere.

It was a plan for celebrating the King's birthday.

Of course, that had been done in many lands before, but there were certain features about this celebration which differed materially from anything that had ever been tried. They decided that on the King's birthday the people should all bring him gifts, but they wanted in some way to let him know that these gifts were the expression of a love on the part of the giver which was pure and true and unselfish, and in order to show that, it was decided that each gift should be a "White Gift."

The King heard about this beautiful plan, and it touched his heart in a wonderful way. He decided that he would do his part to carry out the idea and let his loving subjects know how much he appreciated their thoughtfulness.

You can just imagine the excitement there was all over the land as the King's birthday drew near. All sorts of loving sacrifices had been made and everyone was anxious to make his gift the very best he had to offer. At last the day dawned, and eagerly the people came dressed in white and carrying their white gifts. To their surprise they were ushered into a great, big room—the largest one in the palace. They stood in silence when they first entered it, for it was beautiful beyond all expression. It was a *white* room;—the floor was white marble; the ceiling looked like a mass of soft, white fluffy clouds; the walls were hung with beautiful white silken draperies, and all the furnishings were white. In one end of the room stood a stately white throne, and seated upon it was their beloved ruler and he was clad in shining white robes, and his attendants—all dressed in white—were grouped around him.

Then came the presentation of the gifts. What a wealth of them there was—and how different they were in value. In those days it was just as it is now—there were many people who had great wealth, and they brought gifts which were generous in proportion to their wealth.

One brought a handful of pearls, another a number of carved ivories. There were beautiful laces and silks and embroideries, all in pure white, and even splendid white chargers were brought to his majesty.

But many of the people were poor—some of them very poor—and their gifts were quite different from those I have been telling about. Some of the women brought handfuls of white rice, some of the boys brought their favorite white pigeons, and one dear little girl smilingly gave him a pure white rose.

It was wonderful to watch the King as each one came and kneeled before him as he presented his gift. He never seemed to notice whether the gift was great or small; he regarded not one gift above another so long as all were white. Never had the King been so happy as he was that day and never had such real joy filled the hearts of the people. They decided to use the same plan every year, and so it came to pass that year after year on the King's birthday the people came from here and there and everywhere and brought their white gifts—the gifts which showed that their love was pure, strong, true and without stain, and year after year the King sat in his white robes on the white throne in the great white room and it was always the same—he regarded not one gift above another so long as all were white.

HER BIRTHDAY DREAM*

By Nellie C. King

Marcia Brownlow came out of the church, and walked rapidly down the street. She seemed perturbed; her gray eyes flashed, and on her cheeks glowed two red spots. She was glad she was not going home, so she wouldn't have to take a car, but could walk the short distance to Aunt Sophy's, where she had been invited to dine and visit with her special chum, Cousin Jack—who was home from college for the short Thanksgiving vacation. She slowed up as she reached her destination, and waited a little before going in—she wanted to get calmed down a bit, for she didn't want her friend to see her when she felt so "riled up." Back of it was a secret reluctance to meet Jack—he was so different since the Gipsy Smith revival; of course, he was perfectly lovely, and unchanged toward her, but—somehow, she felt uncomfortable in his presence—and she didn't enjoy having her self-satisfaction disturbed.

As she entered the dining-room, she was greeted with exclamations of surprise and pleasure.

"Why, Marcia!" said Aunt Sophia; "we had given you up! I almost never knew of your being late in keeping an appointment."

"You must excuse me, Auntie; and lay this offense to the charge of our Sunday school superintendent," answered Marcia.

"I suppose Mr. Robinson is laying his plans for Christmas," remarked Uncle John. "He believes in taking time by the forelock—and a very commendable habit it is, too."

"Yes," answered Marcia laconically.

Jack glanced at her keenly. "Is there anything new in the Christmas line?" he asked.

The gray eyes grew black, and the red spots burned again, as Marcia replied: "Well, I should think so—he proposes to turn things topsy-turvy!"

"My! What does he want to do?" inquired Cousin Augusta.

"Oh, he calls it the 'White Gift Christmas'; but the long and short of the matter is, that he proposes to 'turn down' Santa Claus, and all the old time-honored customs connected with Christmas that are so dear to the hearts of the children, and have the school do the giving. He has a big banner hung up in the Sunday school room bearing the words, 'Gifts for the Christ-Child'."

"An excellent idea," exclaimed Uncle John, "but I don't see much of an innovation about that; you have always made the children's giving a part of your Christmas celebration, have you not?"

"Certainly!" rejoined Marcia. "They have always brought their little gifts for the poor, and that is all right; but this time there are no gifts to the Sunday school at all."

"Not even to the Primary School?" asked Augusta.

"Well," admitted Marcia, "Mr. Robinson gave the children their choice today, whether they would have the old Christmas or the 'White Gift Christmas,' and they all voted for the new idea."

"Why then should the children be obliged to have gifts, if they don't want them?" laughed Augusta.

"Oh, children are always taken with novelty, and Mr. Robinson told it to them in such a way that fancy was captivated; but I don't think they really understood what they were giving up."

"Marcia, it seems to me that your are emphasizing the wrong side of the subject if I understand it aright," said Jack.

"Why, do you know about it?" asked Marcia, in surprise.

"Not much," replied Jack; "but I read the White Gift story in the 'Sunday School Times,' and the report of the Painesville experiment."

"Well, Jack, tell us what you know about this mysterious 'White Gift'," commanded his father.

"I would rather Marcia should tell it, father; I know so little."

"Oh, go on, Jack," urged Marcia; "you can't possibly know less about it than I do, for I confess I was so full of the disappointment of the little ones that the other side of it didn't impress me very much."

"Well, as I remember it," said Jack, "the gist of the plan is this— that Christmas is Christ's birthday, and we should make our gifts to him, instead of to one another; and the idea of the White Gift was suggested by the story of the Persian king named Kublah Khan, who was a wise and good ruler, and greatly beloved. On his birthday his subjects kept what they called the 'White Feast.' This was celebrated in an immense great white banqueting-hall, and each one of his subjects brought to their king a white gift to express that the love and loyalty of their hearts was without stain. The rich brought white chargers, ivory and alakaster; the poor brought white pigeons, or even a measure of rice; and the great king regarded all gifts alike, so long as they were white. Have I told it right, cousin?" queried Jack.

"Yes, I think so. It is a beautiful thought, I must confess, and might be all right in a large, rich Sunday school; but in a mission school like ours I am sure it will be a failure. It will end in our losing our scholars. I don't believe in taking up new ideas without considering whether they are adapted to our needs or not. But please, dear folkses, don't let us say anything more about it," pleaded Marcia, and so the subject was dropped.

That evening as Jack Thornton bade his cousin good-bye, he placed in her hand a little package, saying: "I am so sorry, Marcia, that I can't be here for your birthday, but here is my remembrance. Now don't you dare open it before Tuesday, and, dear, you may be sure it is a 'white gift,' and may you have a 'white birthday'." And before she could say a word, he had opened the door, and was gone.

Touched by his thoughtful gift and his words, she said to herself: "A 'white birthday!' I always have perfectly beautiful birthdays."

And so she did; for she was always looking out for other people's birthdays, and making much of them; and so she always got the gospel measure: "Give, and it shall be given unto you; good measure, pressed down, and shaken together, and running over, shall man give into your bosom."

But these thoughts were crowded out by the pressure of things to be done—father and mother had gone into the country to visit a sick friend, and the younger brothers and sisters surrounded her and clamored for songs and Bible stories, and as she was a good older sister she devoted herself to them until their bedtime. Then, turning out the lights, she sat down in an easy chair before the library grate, and yielded herself to the spell of the quiet hour. The strained, irritated nerves relaxed, and a strange, sweet peace stole over her. As she gazed dreamily into the fire, a star seemed to rise out of the glowing coals, and beam at her with a beautiful soft radiance, and the words of the Evangel came into her mind: "And when they saw the star, they rejoiced with exceeding joy; and when they were come into the house they saw the young child, with Mary his mother, and they fell down and worshipped him; and when they had opened their treasures they presented unto him gifts, gold, frankincense and myrrh." She repeated the words over and over to herself. How simple and restful they were; how direct and genuine and satisfying was this old-time giving! There it was—Gifts for the Christ-Child—"They presented unto him gifts, gold, frankincense and myrrh." She remembered reading somewhere that the gold represented our earthly possessions, the frankincense typified our service and the myrrh our suffering for his sake.

As she gazed into the fire, and mused, she fell asleep, and all these thoughts were woven into the fabric of a dream—and who shall say that God does not speak to his children still in dreams?

She dreamed that it was the morning of her birthday. She heard cheery voices in the hall calling out to one another: "This is Marcia's birthday. Wish you many returns of the day!" There was an excited running to and fro between the different rooms, and gleeful exclamations—but no one came near her! She sat up in bed listening, and wondering what it could mean! Why, mother always came into her room, and folded her to her heart, and said those precious things that only a mother can say; and the children always scrambled to see who should be the first to give sister a birthday kiss. Were they playing some joke on her? She would be quiet and watch, and so not be taken unawares.

Presently they went trooping happily downstairs into the dining-room, and she heard father's voice say: "Good morning, children; I wish you many happy returns of Marcia's birthday."

What did it all mean? Was she going crazy? Or were they just going to surprise her by some novel way of celebrating her birthday? She arose, and with trembling fingers dressed herself hastily, and stole softly down the stairs, and looked into the dining-room. Hush!—father was asking a blessing. He returned thanks for dear Marcia's birthday, and asked that it should be a happy day for them all. Beside each plate save her own, were various packages; and these were opened amid ejaculations of surprise and pleasure, and sundry hugs and kisses.

After the first burst of happiness had subsided, Marcia braced herself and entered the dining-room, saying with forced gayety: "Good morning, dear ones all." They looked up with blank, unanswering faces, and said: "Good morning, Marcia"—that was all. But Marcia's heart leaped at the recognition of her presence, for she had begun to fear that she was dead, and that it was her spirit that was wandering about.

She stooped and kissed her mother, who murmured abstractedly, "Yes, dear," never once looking up from the presents she was examining. With a sinking heart she turned away from her mother and went and stood behind her father's chair, and leaning over whispered in his ear: "Dear father, have you forgotten that this is my birthday?" He answered kindly but absent-mindedly: "Why, daughter, am I likely to forget it with all these tokens around me?"—and he waved his hand toward the gifts piled around his plate. This was almost more than Marcia could bear, for father was always specially tender and attentive to her on her birthday. She always sat on his knee a while; and he told her what a joy and comfort she was to him, and he always paid her some pretty compliment that made her girlish heart swell with innocent pride, for every girl knows that compliments from one's father are a little sweeter than any others.

In vain she hung around waiting for some clue to this mysterious, unnatural conduct of the family. They were all absorbed in plans for spending this birthday—Marcia's birthday, but no reference whatever was made to what she liked; no one consulted her as to what she wanted to do, or to have done. The boys were going skating in the forenoon; the little girls were to invite four of their friends to help serve the first dinner in the new doll's house, and in the afternoon father would take them all for an automobile ride into the country to a dear friend's—all but Marcia, who couldn't bear to get into an auto since a terrible accident she had been in a few weeks ago. A troop of her girl friends came in, and in a conventional way wished her "many happy returns" of the day; and then proceeded to ignore her, and gave gifts to other members of the family. "It is a wonder," thought Marcia, bitterly, "that they didn't have a birthday party for Marcia with Marcia left out."

And so it went on all through that strange, miserable day; while they were all busy celebrating her birthday, she herself was neglected and ignored as she sat in the quiet house alone in the twilight—for she had no heart to light the gas—just homesick for the personal love which had characterized all her birthdays and all her home life heretofore, there came a timid knock on the door, and as Marcia opened it, there stood little crippled Joe, one of her scholars in the Mission Sunday school. As he saw her, he gave a little exclamation of surprise and delight, and said: "O Miss Marshay! I hearn last night 'twas yer berthday today, an' I wanted to guv yer suthin' white, like Mr. Robinson he told us 'bout, don't yer know?—an' 'caus yer has allers treated me so white—'n'—'n' I didn't hev nuthin', 'n so I axed Him, ye know, what yer telled us 'bout in Sunday school—Jesus; who died on the cross, and who's allers willin' to help a poor feller—an' I axed Him to help me get suthin' real nice 'n' white fer uer birthday; 'n I kep' me eyes peeled all day 'xpectin' it, 'n just now a reel swell feller buyed a paper of me, 'n then he guv he this here bunch uv white sweet smellin' posies, 'thout my sayin' a word. Here they be, Miss Marshay fer yer. Giminy, teacher, ain't them purty? An' O, teacher—He made 'm in the fust place 'n had the man guv them to me, 'n so I reckon He 'n me's pardners in this here white gift bizness." And he held up in his thin, grimy hand a bunch of white, sweet-scented violets.

Marcia's first impulse was to catch up the little fellow and his gift in her arms, and baptize them with a flood of tears from her own overcharged heart! But she hadn't taught boys in a Mission Sunday school class for nothing—Joe would have thought she had gone crazy, or been struck silly, or was sick unto death; so she controlled herself, and kneeling beside him took the violets reverently in both her hands, saying in a choked voice: "Joe, they are just beautiful! This is the only really truly white gift I have had today, and I don't deserve it—but I thank Him and you."

The boy looked at her with shining face, drew his hand across his eyes, and then answered brightly: "Oh, that's all right, Miss Marshay; 'tenny rate 'tis with me, 'n I reckon 'tis with Him"— and seizing his crutch, he hopped like a little sparrow through the door and onto the street, and she heard his boyish voice calling out: "Evenin' papers, last edishun—all 'bout the big graft 'sposure."

Just then the big white touring car discharged its merry load at the door, and the house was filled with the chatter and laughter of the children. In vain she tried to find a quiet corner where she could be alone with her heart—it was impossible to escape from the hilarious celebration of her birthday. She was so glad when the children said good-night and went off to bed, and she could seek the quiet of her own room.

As she bade her father good night, he said: "Well, daughter, I hope you have enjoyed your birthday and all your gifts?"

At this all the honesty of her nature, all the hatred of sham, rose up in one indignant outburst, and she exclaimed: "I have had no gifts, neither has this been my birthday celebration."

"Why, Marcia!" said her father in an aggrieved tone, "this certainly is your birthday, and we have been very happy in keeping it for love of you."

"I have failed to see any manifestation of love to me," retorted Marcia. "You may have had a happy time, but I have not been in it; you have given gifts to one another, but I have had just one"— and she held up the bunch of violets. "This is a gift of love from little lame Joe, in answer to his prayer, and in pity for my hungry heart."

There was silence in the room for a moment, and then her father answered: "It seems to me, daughter, that when you get right down to a personal application, what you believe in after all is a 'white birthday'."

The words went through her like an electric shock, and with a start she awoke, and sat upright in her chair; and, lo, it was all a dream!

Marcia looked around the room, shook herself a little, stirred the fire, and put on fresh coal. She laughed at the remembrance of her dream, and its absurdity! How glad she was that it was only a dream! But was it only a dream? Was it not a reality? Was not this the way she had kept the Lord's birthday? When she had opened her Christmas treasure, how much had been given Him and for love of Him? How large a place had she given Him in the season's activity? Had she ever made room for Him as the central figure of it all; or had he been crowded out, and His rightful place given to Santa Claus and the world's merry-making?

In the light of the Spirit she saw that the Star of Bethlehem always leads to the cross of Calvary. She had never liked to think about the cross before, but now it was all illumined with the glory of the love which gave to us God's best, his only begotten Son. She remembered how the Lord Jesus had said: "If I be lifted up, I will draw all men unto Me." She saw that it is as we see Christ on the cross for us that we are drawn to Him.

In that still hour, on her knees, at the foot of the cross, Marcia with great gladness made her first "White Gift" unto her Lord—she gave HERSELF to Him.

*By permission of the author and the publisher, Pittsburgh Christian Advocate.

THE FIR TREE*

Adapted by J. H. Stickney

Far away in the forest, where the warm sun and the fresh air made a sweet resting place, grew a pretty little fir tree. The situation was all that could be desired; and yet it was not happy, it wished so much to be like its tall companions, the pines and firs which grew around it.

The sun shone, and the soft air fluttered its leaves, and the little peasant children passed by, prattling merrily; but the fir tree did not heed them.

Sometimes the children would bring a large basket of raspberries or strawberries, wreathed in straws, and seat themselves near the fir tree, and say, "Is it not a pretty little tree?" which made it feel even more unhappy than before.

And yet all this while the tree grew a notch or joint taller every year; for by the number of joints in the stem of a fir tree we can discover its age.

Still, as it grew, it complained: "Oh! how I wish I were as tall as the other trees; then I would spread out my branches on every side, and my crown would overlook the wide world around. I should have the birds building their nests on my boughs, and when the wind blew, I should bow with stately dignity, like my tall companions."

So discontented was the tree, that it took no pleasure in the warm sunshine, the birds, or the rosy clouds that floated over it morning and evening.

Sometimes in winter, when the snow lay white and glittering on the ground, there was a little hare that would come springing along, and jump right over the little tree's head; then how mortified it would feel.

Two winters passed; and when the third arrived, the tree had grown so tall that the hare was obliged to run round it. Yet it remained unsatisfied, and would exclaim, "Oh! to grow, to grow; if I could but keep on growing tall and old! There is nothing else worth caring for in the world."

In the autumn the woodcutters came, as usual, and cut down several of the tallest trees; and the young fir, which was now grown to its full height, shuddered as the noble trees fell to the earth with a crash.

After the branches were lopped off, the trunks looked so slender and bare that they could scarcely be recognized. Then they were placed, one upon another, upon wagons, and drawn by horses out of the forest. "Where could they be going? What would become of them?" The young fir tree wished very much to know.

So in the spring, when the swallows and the storks came, it asked, "Do you know where those trees were taken? Did you meet them?"

The swallows knew nothing; but the stork, after a little reflection, nodded his head, and said, "Yes, I think I do. As I flew from

Egypt, I saw several new ships, and they had fine masts that smelt like fir. These must have been the trees; and I assure you they were stately; they sailed right gloriously!"

"Oh, how I wish I were tall enough to go on the sea," said the fir tree. "Tell me what is this sea, and what does it look like?"

"It would take too much time to explain, a great deal too much," said the stork, flying quickly away.

"Rejoice in thy youth," said the sunbeam; "rejoice in thy fresh growth, and in the young life that is in thee."

And the wind kissed the tree, and the dew watered it with tears; but the fir tree regarded them not.

Christmas time drew near, and many young trees were cut down, some that were even smaller and younger than the fir tree, who enjoyed neither rest nor peace with longing to leave its forest home. These young trees, which were chosen for their beauty, kept their branches, and were also laid on wagons, and drawn by horses far away out of the forest.

"Where are they going?" asked the fir tree. "They are not taller than I am; indeed, one is not so tall. And why do they keep all their branches? Where are they going?"

"We know, we know," sang the sparrows; "we have looked in at the windows of the houses in the town, and we know what is done with them. Oh! you cannot think what honor and glory they receive. They are dressed up in the most splendid manner. We have seen them standing in the middle of a warm room, and adorned with all sorts of beautiful things;—honey cakes, gilded apples, playthings, and many hundreds of wax tapers."

"And then," asked the fir tree, trembling in all its branches, "and then what happens?"

"We did not see any more," said the sparrows; "but this was enough for us."

"I wonder whether anything so brilliant will ever happen to me," thought the fir tree. "It would be better even than crossing the sea. I long for it almost with pain. Oh, when will Christmas be here? I am now as tall and well grown as those which were taken away last year. Oh, that I were now laid on the wagon, or standing in the warm room, with all that brightness and splendor around me! Something better and more beautiful is to come after, or the trees would not be so decked out. Yes, what follows will be grander and more splendid. What can it be? I am weary with longing. I scarcely know what it is that I feel."

"Rejoice in our love," said the air and the sunlight. "Enjoy thine own bright life in the fresh air."

But the tree would not rejoice, though it grew taller every day and, winter and summer, its dark green foliage might be seen in the forests, while passersby would say, "What a beautiful tree!"

A short time before Christmas the discontented fir tree was the first to fall. As the axe cut sharply through the stem, and divided the pith, the tree fell with a groan to the earth, conscious of pain and faintness, and forgetting all its dreams of happiness, in sorrow at leaving its home in the forest. It knew that it should never again see its dear old companions, the trees, nor the little bushes and many-colored flowers that had grown by its side; perhaps not even the birds. Nor was the journey at all pleasant.

The tree first recovered itself while being unpacked in the courtyard of a house, with several other trees; and it heard a man say, "We only want one, and this is the prettiest. This is beautiful!"

Then came two servants in grand livery, and carried the fir tree into a large and beautiful apartment. Pictures hung on the walls, and near the great stove stood great china vases, with lions on the lids. There were rocking chairs, silken sofas, large tables covered with pictures, books, and playthings that had cost a hundred times a hundred dollars; at least so said the children.

Then the fir tree was placed in a large tub, full of sand; but green baize hung all around it, so that no one could know it was a tub; and it stood on a very handsome carpet. Oh, how the fir tree trembled! What was going to happen to him now? Some young ladies came in, and the servants helped them to adorn the tree.

On one branch they hung little bags cut out of colored paper, and each bag was filled with sweetmeats. From other branches hung gilded apples and walnuts, and all around were hundreds of red, blue and white tapers, which were fastened upon the branches. Dolls, exactly like real men and women, were placed under the green leaves,—and the tree had never seen such things before,—and at the top was fastened a glittering star, made of gold tinsel.

Oh, it was very beautiful. "This evening," they all exclaimed, "how bright it will be!"

"Oh, that the evening were come," thought the tree, "and the tapers lighted! Then I should know what else is going to happen. Will the trees of the forest come to see me? Will the sparrows peep in at the windows, I wonder, as they fly? Shall I grow faster here, and keep on all these ornaments during summer and winter?" But guessing was of very little use. His back ached with trying; and this pain is as bad for a slender fir tree as headache is for us.

At last the tapers were lighted, and then what a glistening blaze of splendor the tree presented! It trembled so with joy in all its branches, that one of the candles fell among the green leaves and burnt some of them. "Help! help!" exclaimed the young ladies; but there was no danger, for they quickly extinguished the fire.

After this the tree tried not to tremble at all, though the fire frightened him, he was so anxious not to hurt any of the beautiful ornaments, even while their brilliancy dazzled him.

And now the folding doors were thrown open, and a troop of children rushed in as if they intended to upset the tree, and were followed more slowly by their elders. For a moment the little ones stood silent with astonishment, and then they shouted for joy till the room rang; and they danced merrily round the tree, while one present after another was taken from it.

"What are they doing? What will happen next?" thought the tree. At last the candles burned down to the branches, and were put out. Then the children received permission to plunder the tree.

Oh, how they rushed upon it! There was such a riot that the branches cracked, and had it not been fastened with the glistening star to the ceiling, it must have been thrown down.

Then the children danced about with their pretty toys, and no one noticed the tree, except the children's maid, who came and peeped among the branches to see if an apple or a fig had been forgotten.

"A story, a story," cried the children, pulling a little fat man toward the tree.

"Now we shall be in green shade," said the man, as he seated himself under it, "and the tree will have the pleasure of hearing also; but I shall only relate one story. What shall it be? Ivede-Avede, or Humpty-Dumpty, who fell down stairs, but soon got up again, and at last married a princess?"

"Ivede-Avede," cried some. "Humpty-Dumpty," cried others; and there was a famous uproar. But the fir tree remained quite still, and thought to himself, "Shall I have anything to do with all this? Ought I to make a noise too?" but he had already amused them as much as they wished.

Then the old man told them the story of Humpty-Dumpty;—how he fell downstairs and was raised up again, and married a princess. And the children clapped their hands and cried "Tell another, tell another," for they wanted to hear the story of Ivede-Avede; but this time they had only Humpty-Dumpty. After this the fir tree became quite silent and thoughtful. Never had the birds in the forest told such tales as Humpty-Dumpty who fell down stairs, and yet married a princess.

"Ah, yes! so it happens in the world," thought the fir tree. He believed it all, because it was related by such a pleasant man.

"Ah, well!" he thought, "who knows? Perhaps I may fall down too and marry a princess;" and he looked forward joyfully to the next evening, expecting to be again decked out with lights and playthings, gold and fruit. "Tomorrow I will not tremble," thought he; "I will enjoy all my splendor, and I shall hear the story of Humpty-Dumpty again, and perhaps Ivede-Avede." And the tree remained quiet and thoughtful all night.

In the morning the servants and the housemaid came in. "Now," thought the fir tree, "all my splendor is going to begin again." But they dragged him out of the room and upstairs to the garret and threw him on the floor, in a dark corner where no daylight shone, and there they left him. "What does this mean?" thought the tree. "What am I to do here? I can hear nothing in a place like this;" and he leaned against the wall and thought and thought.

And he had time enough to think, for days and nights passed, and no one came near him; and when at last somebody did come, it was only to push away some large boxes in a corner. So the tree was completely hidden from sight as if it had never existed.

"It is winter now," thought the tree; "the ground is hard and covered with snow, so that people cannot plant me. I shall be sheltered here, I dare say, until spring comes. How thoughtful and kind everybody is to me! Still, I wish this place were not so dark and so dreadfully lonely, with not even a little hare to look at. How pleasant it was out in the forest while the snow lay on the ground, when the hare would run by, yes, and jump over me too, although I did not like it then. Oh! it is terribly lonely here."

"Squeak, squeak," said a little mouse, creeping cautiously towards the tree; then came another, and they both sniffed at the fir tree, and crept in and out between the branches.

"Oh, it is very cold here," said the little mouse. "If it were not, we would be very comfortable here, wouldn't we, old fir tree?"

"I am not old," said the fir tree. "There are many who are older than I am."

"Where do you come from?" asked the mice, who were full of curiosity; "and what do you know? Have you seen the most beautiful places in the world, and can you tell us all about them? And have you been in the storeroom, where cheeses lie on the shelf and hams hang from the ceiling? One can run about on tallow candles there; one can go in thin and come out fat."

"I know nothing of that," said the fir tree; "but I know the wood where the sun shines and the birds sing." And then the tree told the little mice all about its youth. They had never heard such an account in their lives; and after they had listened to it attentively, they said, "What a number of things you have seen! You must have been very happy."

"Happy!" exclaimed the fir tree; and then, as he reflected on what he had been telling them, he said, "Ah, yes! after all, those were happy days." But when he went on and related all about Christmas eve, and how he had been dressed up with cakes and lights, the mice said, "How happy you must have been, you old fir tree."

"I am not old at all," replied the tree; "I only came from the forest this winter. I am now checked in my growth."

"What splendid stories you can tell," said the little mice. And the next night four other mice came with them to hear what the tree had to tell. The more he talked, the more he remembered, and then he thought to himself, "Yes, those were happy days; but they may come again. Humpty-Dumpty fell downstairs, and yet he married a princess. Perhaps I may marry a princess too." And the fir tree thought of the pretty little birch tree that grew in the forest; a real princess, a beautiful princess, she was to him.

"Who is Humpty-Dumpty?" asked the little mice. And then the tree related the whole story; he could remember every single word. And the little mice were so delighted with it, that they were ready to jump to the top of the tree. The next night a great many more mice made their appearance, and on Sunday two rats came with them; but they said it was not a pretty story at all, and the little mice were very sorry, for it made them also think less of it.

"Do you know only that one story?" asked the rats.

"Only that one," replied the fir tree. "I heard it on the happiest evening of my life; but I did not know I was so happy at the time."

"We think it is a very miserable story," said the rats. "Don't you know any story about bacon or tallow in the storeroom?"

"No," replied the tree.

"Many thanks to you, then," replied the rats, and they went their ways.

The little mice also kept away after this, and the tree sighed and said, "It was very pleasant when the merry little mice sat around me and listened while I talked. Now that is all past too. However, I shall consider myself happy when someone comes to take me out of this place."

But would this ever happen? Yes; one morning people came to clear up the garret; the boxes were packed away, and the tree was pulled out of the corner and thrown roughly on the floor; then the servants dragged it out upon the staircase where the daylight shone.

"Now life is beginning again," said the tree, rejoicing in the sunshine and fresh air. Then it was carried downstairs and taken into the courtyard so quickly that it forgot to think of itself, and could only look about, there was so much to be seen.

The court was close to a garden, where everything looked blooming. Fresh and fragrant roses hung over the little palings. The linden trees were in blossom; while the swallows flew here and there crying, "Twit, twit, twit, my mate is coming;" but it was not the fir tree they meant.

"Now I shall live," cried the tree joyfully, spreading out its branches; but alas! they were all withered and yellow, and it lay in a corner amongst weeds and nettles. The star of gold paper still stuck in the top of the tree, and glittered in the sunshine.

In the same courtyard two of the merry children were playing who had danced round the tree at Christmas time and had been so happy. The youngest saw the gilded star and ran and pulled it off the tree. "Look what is sticking to the ugly old fir tree," said the child, treading on the branches till they crackled under his boots.

And the tree saw all the fresh, bright flowers in the garden, and then looked at itself, and wished it had remained in the dark corner of the garret. It thought of its fresh youth in the forest, of the merry Christmas evening, and of the little mice who had listened to the story of Humpty-Dumpty.

"Past! past!" said the poor tree. "Oh, had I but enjoyed myself while I could have done so! but now it is too late."

Then a lad came and chopped the tree into small pieces, till a large bundle lay in a heap on the ground. The pieces were placed in the fire, and they blazed up brightly, while the tree sighed so deeply that each sigh was like a little pistol shot. Then the children, who were at play, came and seated themselves in front of the fire and looked at it, and cried, "Pop, pop." But at each "pop," which was a deep sigh, the tree was thinking of a summer day in the forest, or of some winter night there when the stars shone brightly, and of Christmas evening and of Humpty-Dumpty, the only story it had ever heard, or knew how to relate,—till at last it was consumed.

The boys still played in the garden, and the youngest wore the golden star on his breast with which the tree had been adorned during the happiest evening of its existence. Now all was past; the tree's life was past, and the story also past! for all stories must come to an end some time or other.

*From "Hans Andersen's Fairy Tales," adapted by J. H. Stickney. By permission of the publishers—Ginn and Company.

THE LITTLE MATCH GIRL*

Hans Andersen

It was dreadfully cold; it was snowing fast, and was almost dark, as evening came on—the last evening of the year. In the cold and the darkness, there went along the street a poor little girl, bareheaded and with naked feet. When she left home she had slippers on, it is true; but they were much too large for her feet,—slippers that her mother had used until then, and the poor little girl lost them in running across the street when two carriages were passing terribly fast. When she looked for them, one was not to be found, and a boy seized the other and ran away with it, saying he would use it for a cradle some day, when he had children of his own.

So on the little girl went with her bare feet, that were red and blue with cold. In an old apron that she wore were bundles of matches, and she carried a bundle also in her hand. No one had bought so much as a bunch all the long day, and no one had given her even a penny.

Poor little girl! Shivering with cold and hunger she crept along, a perfect picture of misery!

The snowflakes fell on her long flaxen hair, which hung in pretty curls about her throat; but she thought not of her beauty nor of the cold. Lights gleamed in every window, and there came to her the savory smell of roast goose, for it was New Year's Eve. And it was of this which she thought.

In a corner formed by two houses, one of which projected beyond the other, she sat cowering down. She had drawn under her little feet, but still she grew colder and colder; yet she dared not go home, for she had sold no matches, and could not bring a penny of money. Her father would certainly beat her; and, besides, it was cold enough at home, for they had only the houseroof above them; and, though the largest holes had been stopped with straw and rags, there were left many through which the cold wind whistled.

And now her little hands were nearly frozen with cold. Alas! a single match might do her good if she might only draw it from the bundle, rub it against the wall, and warm her fingers by it. So at last she drew one out. Whischt! How it blazed and burned! It gave out a warm, bright flame like a little candle, as she held her hands over it. A wonderful little light it was. It really seemed to the little girl as if she sat before a great iron stove, with polished brass feet and brass shovel and tongs. So blessedly it burned that the little maiden stretched out her feet to warm them also. How comfortable she was! But lo! the flame went out, the stove vanished. and nothing remained but the little burned match in her hand.

She rubbed another match against the wall. It burned brightly, and where the light fell upon the wall it became transparent like a veil, so that she could see through it into the room. A snow-white cloth was spread upon the table, on which was a beautiful china dinner service, while a roast goose, stuffed with apples and prunes, steamed famously, and sent forth a most savory smell. And what was more delightful still, and wonderful, the goose jumped from the dish, with knife and fork still in its breast, and waddled along the floor straight to the little girl.

But the match went out then, and nothing was left to her but the thick, damp wall.

She lighted another match. And now she was under a most beautiful Christmas tree, larger and far more prettily trimmed than the one she had seen through the glass doors at the rich merchant's. Hundreds of wax tapers were burning on the green branches, and gay figures, such as she had seen in the shop windows, looked down upon her. The child stretched out her hands to them; then the match went out.

Still the lights of the Christmas tree rose higher and higher. She saw them as stars in heaven, and one of them fell, forming a long trail of fire.

"Now some one is dying," murmured the child softly; for her grandmother, the only person who had loved her and who was now dead, had told her that whenever a star falls a soul mounts up to God.

She struck yet another match against the wall, and again it was light; and in the brightness there appeared before her the dear old grandmother, bright and radiant, yet sweet and mild, and happy as she had never looked on earth.

"Oh, grandmother," cried the child, "take me with you. I know you will go away when the match burns out. You, too, will vanish, like the warm stove, the splendid New Year's feast, the beautiful

Christmas Tree." And lest her grandmother should disappear, she rubbed the whole bundle of matches against the wall.

And the matches burned with such a brilliant light that it became brighter than noonday. Her grandmother had never looked so grand and beautiful. She took the little girl in her arms, and both flew together, joyously and gloriously, mounting higher and higher, far above the earth; and for them there was neither hunger, nor cold, nor care;—they were with God.

But in the corner, at the dawn of day, sat the poor girl, leaning against the wall, with red cheeks and smiling mouth,—frozen to death on the last evening of the old year. Stiff and cold she sat, with the matches, one bundle of which was burned.

"She wanted to warm herself, poor little thing," people said. No one imagined what sweet visions she had had, or how gloriously she had gone with her grandmother to enter upon the joys of a new year.

*From "Hans Andersen's Fairy Tales." By permission of publishers—Ginn & Company.

LITTLE PICCOLA*

Suggested by One of Mrs. Celia Thaxter's Poems

"Story-telling is a real strengthening spirit-bath."— *Froebel.*

Piccola lived in Italy, where the oranges grow, and where all the year the sun shines warm and bright. I suppose you think Piccola a very strange name for a little girl; but in her country it was not strange at all, and her mother thought it the sweetest name a little girl ever had.

Piccola had no kind father, no big brother or sister, and no sweet baby to play with and love. She and her mother lived all alone in an old stone house that looked on a dark, narrow street. They were very poor, and the mother was away from home almost every day, washing clothes and scrubbing floors, and working hard to earn money for her little girl and herself. So you see Piccola was alone a great deal of the time; and if she had not been a very happy, contented little child, I hardly know what she would have done. She had no playthings except a heap of stones in the back yard that she used for building houses and a very old, very ragged doll that her mother had found in the street one day.

But there was a small round hole in the stone wall at the back of her yard, and her greatest pleasure was to look through that into her neighbor's garden. When she stood on a stone, and put her eyes close to the hole, she could see the green grass in the garden, and smell the sweet flowers, and even hear the water splashing into the fountain. She had never seen anyone walking in the garden, for it belonged to an old gentleman who did not care about grass and flowers.

One day in the autumn her mother told her that the old gentleman had gone away, and had rented his house to a family of little American children, who had come with their sick mother to spend the winter in Italy. After this, Piccola was never lonely, for all day long the children ran and played and danced and sang in the garden. It was several weeks before they saw her at all, and I am not sure they ever would have done so but one day the kitten ran away, and in chasing her they came close to the wall and saw Piccola's black eyes looking through the hole in the stones. They were a little frightened at first, and did not speak to her; but the next day she was there again, and Rose, the oldest girl, went up to the wall and talked to her a little while. When the children found that she had no one to play with and was very lonely, they talked to her every day, and often brought her fruits and candies, and passed them through the hole in the wall.

One day they even pushed the kitten through; but the hole was hardly large enough for her, and she mewed and scratched and was very much frightened. After that the little boy said he would ask his father if the hole might not be made larger, and then Piccola could come in and play with them. The father had found out that Piccola's mother was a good woman, and that the little girl herself was sweet and kind, so that he was very glad to have some of the stones broken away and an opening made for Piccola to come in.

How excited she was, and how glad the children were when she first stepped into the garden! She wore her best dress, a long, bright-colored woolen skirt and a white waist. Round her neck was a string of beads, and on her feet were little wooden shoes. It would seem very strange to us—would it not?—to wear wooden shoes; but Piccola and her mother had never worn anything else, and never had any money to buy stockings. Piccola almost always ran about barefooted, like the kittens and the chickens and the little ducks. What a good time they had that day, and how glad Piccola's mother was that her little girl could have such a pleasant, safe place to play in, while she was away at work!

By and by December came, and the little Americans began to talk about Christmas. One day, when Piccola's curly head and bright eyes came peeping through the hole in the wall, and they ran to her and helped her in; and as they did so, they all asked her at once what she thought she would have for a Christmas present. "A Christmas present!" said Piccola. "Why, what is that?"

All the children looked surprised at this, and Rose said, rather gravely, "Dear Piccola, don't you know what Christmas is?"

Oh, yes, Piccola knew it was the happy day when the baby Christ was born, and she had been to church on that day and heard the beautiful singing, and had seen the picture of the Babe lying in the manger, with cattle and sheep sleeping round about. Oh, yes, she knew all that very well, but what was a Christmas present?

Then the children began to laugh and to answer her all together. There was such a clatter of tongues that she could hear only a few of the words now and then, such as "chimney," "Santa Claus," "stockings," "reindeer," "Christmas Eve," "candies and toys." Piccola put her hands over her ears and said, "Oh, I can't understand one word. You tell me, Rose." Then Rose told her all about jolly Santa Claus, with his red cheeks and white beard and fur coat, and about his reindeer and sleigh full of toys. "Every Christmas Eve," said Rose, "he comes down the chimney, and fills the stockings of all the good children; so, Piccola, you hang up your stocking, and who knows what a beautiful Christmas present you will find when morning comes!" Of course Piccola thought this was a delightful plan, and was very pleased to hear about it. Then all the children told her of every Christmas Eve they could remember, and of the presents they had had; so that she went home thinking of nothing but dolls and hoops and balls and ribbons and marbles and wagons and kites.

She told her mother about Santa Claus, and her mother seemed to think that perhaps he did not know there was any little girl in that house, and very likely he would not come at all. But Piccola felt very sure Santa Claus would remember her, for her little friends had promised to send a letter up the chimney to remind him.

Christmas Eve came at last. Piccola's mother hurried home from her work; they had their little supper of soup and bread, and soon it was bedtime,—time to get ready for Santa Claus. But oh! Piccola remembered then for the first time that the children had told her she must hang up her stocking, and she hadn't any, and neither had her mother.

How sad, how sad it was! Now Santa Claus would come, and perhaps be angry because he couldn't find any place to put the present.

The poor little girl stood by the fireplace, and the big tears began to run down her cheeks. Just then her mother called to her, "Hurry, Piccola; come to bed." What should she do? But she stopped crying, and tried to think; and in a moment she remembered her wooden shoes, and ran off to get one of them. She put it close to the chimney, and said to herself, "Surely Santa Claus will know what it's there for. He will know I haven't any stockings, so I gave him the shoe instead."

Then she went off happily to her bed, and was asleep almost as soon as she had nestled close to her mother's side.

The sun had only just begun to shine, next morning, when Piccola awoke. With one jump she was out on the floor and running toward the chimney. The wooden shoe was lying where she had left it, but you could never, never guess what was in it.

Piccola had not meant to wake her mother, but this surprise was more than any little girl could bear and yet be quiet; so she danced to the bed with the shoe in her hand, calling, "Mother, mother! look, look! see the present Santa Claus brought me!"

Her mother raised her head and looked into the shoe. "Why, Piccola," she said, "a little chimney swallow nestling in your shoe? What a good Santa Claus to bring you a bird!"

"Good Santa Claus, dear Santa Claus!" cried Piccola; and she kissed her mother and kissed the bird and kissed the shoe, and even threw kisses up the chimney, she was so happy.

When the birdling was taken out of the shoe, they found that he did not try to fly, only to hop about the room; and as they looked closer, they could see that one of his wings was hurt a little. But the mother bound it up carefully, so that it did not seem to pain him, and he was so gentle that he took a drink of water from a cup, and even ate crumbs and seeds out of Piccola's hands. She was a proud little girl when she took her Christmas present to show the children in the garden. They had had a great many gifts,— dolls that could say "mamma," bright picture books, trains of cars, toy pianos; but not one of their playthings was alive, like Piccola's birdling. They were as pleased as she, and Rose hunted about the house until she found a large wicker cage that belonged to a blackbird she once had. She gave the cage to Piccola, and the swallow seemed to make himself quite at home in it at once, and sat on the perch winking his bright eyes at the children. Rose had saved a bag of candies for Piccola, and when she went home at last, with the cage and her dear swallow safely inside it, I am sure there was not a happier little girl in the whole country of Italy.

*From "The Story Hour," by Wiggins and Smith. Published by consent of the authors and also the publishers—Houghton, Mifflin and Company.

THE SHEPHERD'S STORY*

Washington Gladden

"Bring hither that sheepskin, Joseph, and lay it down on this bank of dry earth, under this shelving rock. The wind blows chilly from the west, but the rock will shelter us. The sky is fair and the moon is rising, and we can sit here and watch the flocks on the hillside below. Your young blood and your father's coat of skins will keep you warm for one watch, I am sure. At midnight, my son, your father, Reuben, and his brother James will take our places; for the first watch the old man and the boy will tend the sheep."

"Yes, grandfather; you shall sit in that snug corner of the rock, where you can lean back and take your comfort. I will lie here at your feet. Now and then I will run to see whether the sheep are wandering, and that will warm me, if I grow cold."

"Have you never been out on the hills at night with your father?"

"Never, grandfather. I have often begged him to let me come; but he kept saying that I must wait until I was twelve years old. On the last full moon was my birthday and today, when he returned from Bethlehem to the flocks, he brought me with him."

"So this is the lad's first night with the sheep in the fields, and the old man's last night, I fear," said the aged shepherd, sadly. "It is not often in these days that I venture out to keep the watches of the flock; but this one night of the year I have spent upon these hills these many years, and I always shall as long as I have strength to walk so far."

"Was your father, too, a shepherd?"

"Yes, and all his fathers before him for many generations. On these hills my ancestors have kept their sheep for I know not how long."

Joseph was still for a moment. His eyes wandered away over the silent hills, lit by the rising moon. His face was troubled. At length, he said gently:

"Grandfather, I heard Rabbi Eliezer saying, the other day, in the synagogue, that a shepherd's life is not a noble life. He was reading from one of the old doctors, who said: 'Let no one make his son a camel-driver, a barber, a sailor, a shepherd, or a shopkeeper. They are dishonest callings.' I was angry when he read it; but I held my peace."

"You did well, my son, to hold your peace. I myself have often heard such words, of late, from the doctors in the synagogues; but it is not wise to answer them. Where they got their notions, I know not. From the Egyptians, I think, more than from the prophets. All Egyptians hate shepherds, and can never speak of them without sneering. Perhaps they have not yet forgotten how the shepherds conquered and ruled them for generations. Nevertheless, there is some reason why the calling of the shepherds should be despised. Many of them are rude and fierce men. Living out of doors so constantly makes their manners rough and their temper harsh. They are often quarrelsome. Such bloody fights as I used to see among them, at the wells in the south country, where they brought their flocks to water and each one wanted the first chance at the well, I hope you will never look upon."

"But all shepherds are not so," protested Joseph.

"No, indeed. Brave men they must be; fleet of foot and strong of limb and stout of heart; but brave men are not always quarrelsome. Many a shepherd whom I have known had a heart as pure and gentle as a child's. And the godliest men that I have known have been among them. If the shepherd has but learned to think, to commune with his own soul, he has time for thought and time for prayer. More than one with whom I have watched upon these hills knew all the Psalms of David by heart and many of the books of the prophets. The doctors in the synagogues teach only the law; the shepherds love best the Psalms and the prophets. They do not forget that King David was himself a shepherd's lad. It was upon these very hills that he kept his father's sheep. It was in that ravine over yonder, on that hillside, that he, a mere stripling, caught by the beard and killed the lion and the bear that attacked the sheep. It was on that slope, just a little to the south, that the messenger found him with his flocks when he was called home to be anointed by Samuel the prophet. When the doctors talk so contemptuously about the shepherds, I wonder if they do not remember that the great king wrote: 'The Lord is my Shepherd.' How can our calling be so mean as they say, when David, who was called from the sheepfolds, praises the Eternal One himself as his Shepherd? But hark! what noise is that I hear? There is some trouble among the sheep."

"Let me run and see," answers the boy, "and I will come and bring you word."

So saying, Joseph cast off his father's shaggy coat, seized the sling in his left hand and the crook in his right and ran swiftly out to the brow of the hill. He was a strong lad, large of frame and a swift runner, and the sling in his hand was a sure weapon. The old man looked after him with pride, as he bounded over the rocks, and said to himself:

"Some evil beast, I doubt not. But the lad's heart is brave and he must learn to face dangers. I will wait a moment."

Presently the sheep came huddling round the hill in terror. The quick, faint bleat of the ewes showed that they had seen a foe. The old man arose and hurried in the direction in which the lad had disappeared. Joseph was just returning, breathless, from the ravine below.

"It was a wolf, grandfather. The sheep on this side of the ledge had seen him and were flying. Just as I reached the brow of the hill, he was creeping round the end of the ledge below, ready to spring upon a ewe that was feeding near. The first thing he knew a stone from my sling hit him, and he went howling down the hill. I think I broke his leg, for he went on three legs and I gained on him as I ran after him; but he crawled into a narrow place among the rocks in the gorge down yonder, and I could not follow him."

"Well done, my lad," said the ancient Stephanus proudly. "You will make a good shepherd. These single wolves are cowards. It is always safe to face them. When they come in packs, it is quite another thing. But this fellow will keep at a safe distance for the rest of the night, you may depend. Let us go back to our shelter and call the sheep together."

It was several minutes before Stephanus and Joseph could collect the sheep that the wolf had scattered; but at length, with the aid of the dog, who was not a very brave specimen, and who had taken to his heels when he saw the wolf coming, they succeeded in driving them into a safe neighborhood, and then, with their blood quickened by the adventure, they sat down again beneath the overhanging rock.

"You said, grandfather, that you always spent this night with the flocks in the fields. Why this night?" asked the boy.

"Do you not know, my boy, that this is the night of the year on which the Lord Christ was born?"

"Oh! yes," answered the lad. "My father told me as we were walking hither today, but I had forgotten it. And you were with the sheep that night?"

"Aye."

"Where was it?"

"Here, on this very spot."

The boy's eyes began to grow and fill with wonder and there was a slight tremor in his voice as he hurriedly plied the aged man with his eager questions. Stephanus drew his shepherd's cloak around him, and leaned forward a little, and looked out upon the silent moonlit hills, and then up into the sky.

"How long ago was that, grandfather?"

"Just fifty years ago this night."

"And how old were you then?"

"Fourteen, and a stout boy for my age. I had been for two years in the fields with my father, and had tasted to the full the hardships and dangers of the shepherd's life."

"Who were with you on that night?"

"My father, and his brother, James, and Hosea, the son of John, a neighbor and kinsman of ours. On that year, as on this year and often, there came in the midwinter a dry and warm season between the early and the latter rain. We had driven forth our flocks from Bethlehem and were dwelling by night in the shelter of the tower on the hillside yonder, watching and sleeping two and two. My father and I were wont to keep the early watches. At midnight we would call James and Hosea, and they would watch till the morning. But that night, when the sun went down and the stars came out, we were sitting here, upon this hillside, talking of the troubles of Israel and of the promises of deliverance spoken by the prophets; and James and Hosea were asking my father questions, and he was answering them, for he was older than they, and all the people of Bethlehem reverenced him as a wise and devout man. Some even said that, if the people of Israel had not ceased to look for prophets, they would have counted him a prophet.

47

I remember well that, when he rose in the synagogue, it seemed as if some wisdom from on high touched his lips, and he would speak with such hope and courage of the light that should yet shine in our darkness and of the help that should yet arise to Judah, that the people's faces would glow with joyful expectation."

Stephanus paused a moment and started forward, as his eye was turned toward his own shadow upon the rock, cast by the rising moon. Did the old man's figure that he saw remind him of the patriarch of whom he was talking?

Soon he went on.

"Ah! but they should have heard my father talking here by night, under the stars. It was here upon these hills where the royal shepherd used to sing, that his tongue was loosed and he spoke wonderful words. So it was that night, fifty years ago. I remember it as if it were yesterday. My father sat in this very niche, where I am sitting now; James and Hosea were on either side of him. I was lying at their feet, as you now lie at mine. Their faces kindled and the tremor of deep feeling was in their voices as they talked together; and the other two had lingered here three or four hours after the sun had set. It was not a moonlit night like this, but all the stars were out and all the winds were still.

"Suddenly I saw my father rise to his feet. Then the other men sprang up, with astonishment and wonder upon their faces. It had grown light all at once, lighter than the brightest moon; and as I turned my face in the direction in which the others were looking, I saw, standing there upon that level place, a figure majestic and beautiful beyond all the power of words to tell."

"Were you not afraid, grandfather?"

"Indeed, I was, my boy. My heart stopped beating. The others were standing, but I had no power to rise. I lay there motionless upon the earth. My eyes were fixed upon that wonderful face; upon those clear, shining eyes; upon that brow that seemed to beam with the purity of the soul within. It was not a smile with which that face was lighted. It was something too noble and exalted to call by that name. It was a look that told of power and peace, of joy and triumph."

"Did you know that it was an angel?"

"I knew not anything. I only knew that what I saw was glorious, too glorious for mortal eyes to look upon. Yet, while I gazed, and in far less time than I have now taken to tell you of what I saw, the terribleness of the look began to disappear, the sweetness and grace of the soul shone forth, and I had almost ceased to tremble before the angel opened his mouth. And when he spoke, his voice, clearer than any trumpet and sweeter than any lute, charmed away all my fears."

"'Be not afraid' he said, 'for behold I bring you good tidings of great joy which shall be to all people. For there is born to you this day, in the City of David, a Savior, which is Messiah, the King. And this is the sign unto you. Ye shall find a babe wrapped in swaddling clothes and lying in a manger.'

"Oh! that voice, my boy! It makes my heart beat now to remember its sweetness. It seemed to carry these words into our innermost hearts; to print them on our memory, so that we never could forget one syllable of what he said. And then, before we had time to make reply, he turned aside a little and lifted his face toward heaven, and, in a tone far louder than that in which he had spoken to us, but yet so sweet that it did not startle us at all, came forth from his lips the first strain of the great song:

"'Glory to God in the highest!'

"When he had uttered that, he paused a moment, and the echoes, one after another, from hills that were near and hills that were far away, came flying home to us; so that I knew for once what the prophet meant when he said that all the mountains and the hills should break forth into singing. But before the echoes had all faded we began to hear other voices above our heads, a great chorus, taking up the strain that the angel first had sung. At first it seemed dim and far away; but gradually it came nearer, and filled all the air, filled all the earth, filled all our souls with a most entrancing sweetness. Glory to God in the highest!—that was the grandest part. It seemed as though there could be no place so high that that strain would not mount up to it, and no place so happy that that voice would not make it thrill with new gladness. But then came the softer tones, less grand, but even sweeter: 'Peace on earth; good will to men.'

"Oh! my boy, if you had heard that music as I did, you would not wonder when I tell you that it has been hard for me to wait here, in the midst of the dreary noises of earth, for fifty years before hearing it again. But earth that night was musical as heaven. You should have heard the echoes that came back, when the angels' chorus ceased, from all these mountains and all these little hills on every side. There is music enough even in this world, if one can only call it forth; chords divine that will vibrate with wonderful harmony. It only needs an angel's hand to touch the trembling strings."

"Did you see the choir of angels overhead, grandfather?"

"Nay, I saw nothing. The brightness was too dazzling for mortal eyes. We all stood there, with downcast eyes, listening spell-bound to the wonderful melody, until the chorus ceased, and the echoes, one after another, died away, and the glory faded out of the sky and the stars came back again, and no sound was heard but the faint voice of a young lamb, calling for its mother.

"The first to break the silence was my father. 'Come,' he said, in a solemn voice. 'Let us go at once to Bethlehem, and see this thing which is come to pass, which the Lord hath made known unto us.'

"So the sheep were quietly gathered into the fold at the tower, and we hastened to Bethlehem. Never shall I forget that journey by night. We spake not many words, as we traveled swiftly the twenty furlongs; talk seemed altogether tame; but now and then my father broke forth in a song, and the others joined in the chorus. We were not so spent with running but that we could find voice for singing; and such words as these of the prophet were the only ones that could give voice to our swelling hearts:

"Sing, O heavens; and be joyful, O earth;And break forth into singing, O mountains;For the Lord hath comforted His people,And will have mercy on His afflicted.

"How beautiful upon the mountainsAre the feet of Him that bringeth good tidings,That publisheth peace,That bringeth good tidings of good,That publisheth salvation.'

"It was midnight when we climbed the hill to the little city of Bethlehem; the constellation Cesil, called by the Greeks Orion, was just setting in the west. We knew not whither to go. We had only the sign of the angel by which we should know the infant Messiah. He was a babe of one day. He was lying in a manger.

"'Let us go to the inn Chimham,' said my father. 'It stands on the very spot where King David was born. Peradvanture we shall find him there.'

"Over the entrance to the court of the inn a lantern was swinging from a rope stretched across from post to post. Guided by its light, we entered, and found the courtyard full of beasts of burden, showing that the inn was crowded with travelers. In the arched shelter of the hostelry as many as could find room were lying; some who could not sleep were sitting up and waiting drearily for the morning. Two aged women near the entrance, were talking in a low tone.

"'Peace be unto you!' said my father.

"'The Lord be gracious unto thee,' answered the oldest woman, in a solemn voice, as she looked upon my father's white beard; 'but,' she quickly added, 'there is scanty cheer in this place for late comers.'

"'We seek not lodging,' said my father; 'but know you whether among these guests is an infant born this day?'

"'Verily there is,' answered the aged dame; 'a man-child more beautiful than any my eyes have ever beheld. He is lying in a manger there in the cave that serves for stable.'

"We hastened to the mouth of the cave, and there beheld our King. The oxen and the asses were lying near, and a strong man, with a grave and benignant face, was leaning on his staff above the manger. A beautiful young mother lay close beside it, her cheek resting on her hands, that were clasped over the edge of the rock-hewn crib. Into this a little straw had been thrown, and over it a purple robe had been cast, whereon the infant lay. A lamp, set upon a projection of the wall of the cave, burned brightly near. The great eyes of the wonderful child were wandering about the room; his hand touched his mother's lips. I waited to hear him open his mouth and speak.

"There was a moment of silence after we entered the cave. My father broke it with his salutation:

"'Hail, thou blessed among women!' he cried. 'This child of thine is a Prince and a Savior.'

"And then we all bowed low upon our faces before him and worshipped him with praise and gladness.

"The two aged women, with whom we had spoken, had followed us to the door of the stable, and, seeing us worshipping there, had run to call others who were awake in the inn, so that when we arose quite a company were standing at the door, or just within, gazing upon the King in his beauty and listening to our thanksgiving with great wonder.

"Then my father told them all the things that we had heard and seen—the message of the angel, the song in the air, the glory of the Lord that had appeared to us—and how we had quickly come to Bethlehem, and had found things as the angel had told us. 'And it is even,' he cried, 'as the prophet himself hath spoken: "Thou Bethlehem Ephratah, though thou be little among the thousands of Judah, yet out of thee shall he come forth unto me that is to be ruler in Israel, whose going forth hast been of old; even from everlasting."'

"All that heard were full of astonishment—all save the mother. I saw no wonder on her face; the great things that my father told caused her no astonishment; she listened with a quiet and solemn joy, like one who was saying in her heart: 'I knew it all before.'

"When my father had finished speaking, we all bowed low again before the young child; and the mother lifted him in her arms and placed his cheek against her own, smiling graciously on us, but uttering no word. And we came forth from the stable and stood again beneath the stars in the courtyard of the inn. By this time many of the travelers were awake, and an eager company had gathered around us, all of whom desired to be told of the sign that had been shown to us. To one and another we rehearsed our story, lingering long to make known the good tidings, until the morning star appeared and the dawn began to kindle over the eastern hills. Then we hastened to our own homes in the city, and told our kindred what had happened unto us. In the early morning we came back again unto our pastures and our flocks, rejoicing to stand again in the place where the glory of God had shone and the music of heaven had filled the air."

Stephanus paused, his face all aglow with the tale that he had been telling. His eyes swept again the circuit of the moonlit hills and were lifted reverently up to the sky.

"Did you ever see the Lord Christ after that?" asked Joseph.

"Once only. My father and I were at Jerusalem at the passover. It was the year before my father died, seventeen years ago; it was the same week on which our Lord was crucified. My father was then an aged man—fourscore and five years old. Our tent was pitched on the slope of the Mount of Olives, near the Bethany road. While we sat there one morning, a great noise of shouting was heard, and presently we saw one riding on an ass, followed by a great company, crying 'Hosanna!' As we drew nearer, we heard them say that it was Jesus of Nazareth; and, when we saw His face, we knew that it was He, by the wonderful eyes, though it was the face of a bearded man, and not of an infant, and was very pale and sad. As He drew near to our tent, the city came full into His view, with its gilded roofs and marble pinnacles, blazing under the morning sun. Suddenly He paused in the way, and we heard Him weeping aloud, though we could not hear His words of lamentation. The multitude halted, too, when we did; and the cheering ceased, and some of those who stood nearest Him wept also, though no one seemed to know what had caused His grief. But soon they went on again, and before they reached the foot of the hill another multitude met them, coming forth from the city, and we heard their shouts of 'Hosanna in the Highest!' as they entered the gate of Jerusalem."

"What said your father when he saw all this?" queried Joseph.

"He said but little. There was a shadow on his face, yet he spoke cheerfully. 'I cannot understand it,' he murmured. 'They are trying to make Him King of the Jews; but King He will not be, at least not in their fashion. Yet in some way I know He will be Prince and Deliverer. I cannot understand, I will wait.'"

"Were you not in Jerusalem when He was put to death?"

"No. My father was frail and ill and we had hastened home to Bethlehem. News of His death on the cross had only just reached us when another messenger came to tell us that the sepulcher in which He had been laid was empty; that He had risen from the dead.

"My father's eyes kindled when he heard this message. He cast aside his staff and stood firm on his feet. His voice, when he spoke, rang out like a trumpet. 'Blessed be the Lord God of Israel!' he cried. It is thus that He redeemeth His people. This Jesus is not to be the Captain of our armies, but the Savior of our souls. His kingdom is the kingdom of righteousness, and therefore it is that the prophet hath said: "Of the increase of His government and peace there shall be no end."

"Always after that, words of the prophet concerning the Messiah kept coming back to my father; and once and again he cried out: 'Truly, this Jesus was the Son of God, the true King of Israel!' As the months wore on, his words were more and more of the crucified and risen Lord, and he dwelt in a great peace. At length, when the flocks were led forth to the midwinter pasturage, he begged to go with me. It was on this very day that we came, the same day of the year on which the Lord was born. He was feeble and tottered as he walked; but he leaned on my arm and we came slowly. In the evening he said: 'Let me go, my son, and sit once more under the great rock.' I wrapped him in my coat of skins, and sat here where I sit now and where he was sitting when the angel came. We talked here long, under the stars, that night, of Him whom we had learned to love as Master and Lord, of the works that He had done and the words that He had spoken, as His disciples had told of them. We had been silent for a few moments, when I looked up, and saw that his head had fallen backward against the rock wall. I sprang to him. His eyes were shut, but his lips were moving. I put my ear to his mouth, and heard him say only: 'Peace—on—earth—good will'—they were his last words. He had gone beyond our starlight, into the country where the light always shines—the glory that fell that night, fifty years ago, upon these hills of Bethlehem."

Stephanus was silent and Joseph's eyes were full of tears. At length the old man rose.

"Come, my son," he said. "Cesil is in the south; it is midnight; let us call your father and his brother. The old man and the boy have kept their watch, and it is now time for rest."

*Used by permission of the Author.

THE STORY OF CHRISTMAS*

Nora A. Smith

"A great spiritual efficiency lies in story-telling".— *Froebel.*

Christmas Day, you know, dear children, is Christ's day, Christ's birthday, and I want to tell you why we love it so much, and why we try to make every one happy when it comes each year.

A long, long time ago—more than eighteen hundred years—the baby Christ was born on Christmas Day; a baby so wonderful and so beautiful, who grew up to be a man so wise, so good, so patient and sweet that, every year, the people who know about Him love Him better and better, and are more and more glad when His birthday comes again. You see that He must have been very good and wonderful; for people have always remembered His birthday, and kept it lovingly for eighteen hundred years.

He was born, long years ago, in a land far, far away across the seas.

Before the baby Christ was born, Mary, His mother, had to make a long journey with her husband, Joseph. They made this journey to be taxed or counted; for in those days this could not be done in the town where people happened to live, but they must be numbered in the place where they were born.

In that far-off time the only way of traveling was on a horse, or a camel, or a good, patient donkey. Camels and horses cost a great deal of money, and Mary was very poor; so she rode on a quiet, safe donkey, while Joseph walked by her side, leading him and

---

leaning on his stick. Mary was very young, and beautiful, I think, but Joseph was a great deal older than she.

People dress nowadays, in those distant countries, just as they did so many years ago, so we know that Mary must have worn a long, thick dress, falling all about her in heavy folds, and that she had a soft white veil over her head and neck, and across her face. Mary lived in Nazareth, and the journey they were making was to Bethlehem, many miles away.

They were a long time traveling, I am sure; for donkeys are slow, though they are so careful, and Mary must have been very tired before they came to the end of their journey.

They had traveled all day, and it was almost dark when they came near to Bethlehem, to the town where the baby Christ was to be born. There was the place they were to stay,—a kind of inn, or lodging-house, but not at all like those you know about.

They have them today in that far-off country, just as they built them so many years ago.

It was a low, flat-roofed, stone building, with no windows and only one large door. There were no nicely furnished bed rooms inside, and no soft white beds for the tired travelers; there were only little places built into the stones of the wall, something like the berths on steamboats nowadays, and each traveler brought his own bedding. No pretty garden was in front of the inn, for the road ran close to the very door, so that its dust lay upon the doorsill. All around the house, to a high, rocky hill at the back, a heavy stone fence was built, so that the people and the animals inside might be kept safe.

Mary and Joseph could not get very near the inn; for the whole road in front was filled with camels and donkeys and sheep and cows, while a great many men were going to and fro, taking care of the animals. Some of these people had come to Bethlehem to pay their taxes, as Mary and Joseph had done, and others were staying for the night on their way to Jerusalem, a large city a little further on.

The yard was filled, too, with camels and sheep; and men were lying on the ground beside them, resting and watching and keeping them safe. The inn was so full and the yard was so full of people that there was no room for anybody else, and the keeper had to take Joseph and Mary through the house and back to the high hill, where they found another place that was used for a stable. This had only a door and front, and deep caves were behind, stretching far into the rocks.

This was the spot where Christ was born. Think how poor a place!— but Mary was glad to be there, after all; and when the Christ-child came, He was like other babies, and had so lately come from heaven that He was happy everywhere.

There were mangers all around the cave, where the cattle and sheep were fed, and great heaps of hay and straw were lying on the floor. Then, I think, there were brown-eyed cows and oxen there, and quiet, woolly sheep, and perhaps even some dogs that had come in to take care of the sheep.

And there in the cave, by and by, the wonderful baby came, and they wrapped Him up and laid Him in a manger.

All the stars in the sky shone brightly that night, for they knew the Christ-child was born, and the angels in heaven sang together for joy. The angels knew about the lovely child, and were glad that He had come to help the people on earth to be good.

There lay the beautiful baby, with a manger for His bed, and oxen and sheep all sleeping quietly round Him. His mother watched Him and loved Him, and by and by many people came to see Him, for they had heard that a wonderful child was to be born in Bethlehem. All the people in the inn visited Him, and even the shepherds left their flocks in the fields and sought the child and His mother.

But the baby was very tiny, and could not talk any more than any other tiny child, so He lay in His mother's lap, or in the manger, and only looked at the people. So after they had seen Him and loved Him, they went away again.

After a time, when the baby had grown larger, Mary took Him back to Nazareth, and there He lived and grew up.

And He grew to be such a sweet, wise, loving boy, such a tender, helpful man, and He said so many good and beautiful things, that everyone who knew Him, loved Him. Many of the things He said are in the Bible, you know, and a great many beautiful stories of the things He used to do while He was on earth.

He loved little children like you very much, and often used to take them up in His arms and talk to them.

And this is the reason we love Christmas Day so much, and try to make everybody happy when it comes around each year. This is the reason; because Christ, who was born on Christmas Day, has helped us all to be good so many, many times, and because He was the best Christmas present the world ever had!

*From "The Story Hour," by Kate Douglas Wiggins and Nora A. Smith. Used by permission of the authors and also of the publishers—Houghton, Mifflin and Company.

THE LEGEND OF THE CHRISTMAS TREE*

By Lucy Wheelock

Two little children were sitting by the fire one cold winter's night. All at once they heard a timid knock at the door, and one ran to open it.

There, outside in the cold and the darkness, stood a child with no shoes upon his feet and clad in thin, ragged garments. He was shivering with cold, and he asked to come in and warm himself.

"Yes, come," cried both the children; "you shall have our place by the fire. Come in!"

They drew the little stranger to their warm seat and shared their supper with him, and gave him their bed, while they slept on a hard bench.

In the night they were awakened by strains of sweet music and, looking out, they saw a band of children in shining garments approaching the house. They were playing on golden harps, and the air was full of melody.

Suddenly the Stranger Child stood before them; no longer cold and ragged, but clad in silvery light.

His soft voice said: "I was cold and you took Me in. I was hungry, and you fed Me. I was tired, and you gave Me your bed. I am the Christ Child, wandering through the world to bring peace and happiness to all good children. As you have given to Me, so may this tree every year give rich fruit to you."

So saying, He broke a branch from the fir tree that grew near the door, and He planted it in the ground and disappeared. But the branch grew into a great tree, and every year it bore wonderful golden fruit for the kind children.

*From "For the Children's Hour," by Bailey and Lewis. Used by permission of the authors and the publishers—Milton Bradley Company.

LITTLE JEAN*

A Christmas Story

Long ago, and far from here, in a country with a name too hard to pronounce, there lived a little boy named Jean. In many ways, he was just like the boys here, for there are many Johns over here, are there not? Then too, Jean lived with his auntie, and some of our boys do that too. His father and mother were dead, and that is true here sometimes, isn't it? But in some ways things were quite different with Jean. In the first place his auntie was very, very cross, and she often made him climb up his ladder to his little garret room to go to sleep on his pallet of straw, without any supper, save a dry crust. His stockings had holes in the heels, and toes and knees, because his auntie never had time to mend them, and his shoes would have been worn out all the time if they had not been such strong wooden shoes—for in that country the boys all wore wooden shoes. Jean did many a little service around the place, for his auntie made him work for his daily bread, and he chopped the wood and swept the paths and made the fires and ran the errands, but he never heard anyone say "Thank you."

Jean's happiest days were at school, and I wonder if he was like our boys in that? There his playmates wore much better clothes and good stockings too, and warm top coats, but they never thought of making fun of Jean, for they all loved to play with him. One morning Jean started off to school (which was next to the big church), and when he got there he found the children all so happy and gay and dressed in their best clothes, and he heard one boy say, "Won't it be jolly tomorrow with the big tree full of oranges

---

66

and popcorn and candy, and the candles burning?" And another added, "Won't it be fun to see the things in our shoes in the morning, the goodies that boys love?" And another said, "My, but we have a big, fat goose at our house, stuffed with plums and just brown to a turn," and he smacked his lips as he thought of it. And Jean began to wonder about that beautiful tree and wish that one would grow at his house. And he thought about his wooden shoes and knew there would be no goodies in them for him in the morning. Then he heard one boy say, "Don't you love Christmas?" And Jean said, "Christmas! why, what is Christmas?" But just then the teacher came in and said, "Boys, come into the church now and hear the music." And so the boys marched one behind the other just as they do in school here, and they went into the great church. Jean thought it was beautiful in there! The soft light, the warm pleasant air, the flowers, and the marble altar, and then the music! Oh, such music Jean had never heard, and somehow as he sat on the high-backed bench and listened, his own heart grew very warm although he could not understand why, and he loved so to hear them singing: "Peace on earth, good will to men." And it began to sing itself over and over in his heart, this sweet, sweet song of "Peace on earth, good will to men." Then the time came to go home, and the boys all shouted, "Good-bye, Jean! and Merry Christmas!" And though Jean didn't know about "Merry Christmas," he kept singing in his little warmed heart, "Peace on earth, good will to men," and then he was glad the other boys could have the tree and the goose and the wooden shoes full of goodies even if he couldn't.

As Jean went home the snow began to fall and the big flakes lodged on his shoulders and cap and hands, but he didn't mind the cold for his heart was so warm. By and by as he ran down the street he passed a tall house with the steps going up from the street, and there sitting on the bottom step he saw a little boy with soft curling hair and a beautiful face, leaning his head against the stone house, fast asleep. Somehow as Jean looked at the sleeping face, his own heart grew still and quiet and warm, and he felt like he could look at it forever, and suddenly he caught himself singing softly under his breath, "Peace on earth, good will to men." And then he looked down at the little boy's feet and he saw that he was barefooted and his little feet were purple with the cold. As Jean looked at the feet, and then at the face of the child, and thought of the sweet song in his heart, he said, "Oh! I wish I could give him my shoes, for I have stockings to keep me warm, but auntie would be so mad! And the more he looked and thought, the more he longed to give his shoes away, until all at once he said, "I know what I'll do, I'll give him one shoe and one stocking and then he won't be so cold," and he felt as though he couldn't get his shoe and stocking off fast enough to give them to the little child. So gently and tenderly he lifted the little cold foot in his hand to put on the shoe that he did not waken the sleeping boy, even when he had put the stocking on the other foot, and then as he stood up again and took a last look at the lovely face, before he knew it he was singing aloud, "Peace on earth, good will to men." Then he hopped off home in the snow with the happiest heart he had ever had.

Now, I wish the story turned out differently and that his auntie said when he told her about it, "I'm so glad you did it, Jean." But she was so very cross, that she slapped Jean and sent him off to bed without any supper, saying, "You had no right to give away that shoe and stocking for my money paid for them!" Somehow Jean didn't mind doing without supper that night and he soon went fast asleep and dreamed a beautiful dream, for he thought he was still singing "Peace on earth, good will to men!" And he saw a vision of the little sleeping boy, that grew into a tall and gentle man with a radiant face who walked to and fro in Jean's dream, singing with him "Peace on earth, good will to men!" Then morning came and outside his window, Jean heard the voices of children singing, "Glory to God in the highest, on earth peace, good will to men!" And he heard a very strange sound too, for his auntie's voice, soft and gentle, said, "Jean, wake up, and come down and see what has happened," and Jean came down the ladder and lo! there was a wonderful tree just like the other boys were having today, and a goose, and by the fireplace his own wooden shoe, and beside it the mate that he had given to the sleeping child, and far in the distance Jean heard the children's voices singing as they ran down the street, "Peace, peace on earth, good will to men!" Then the room grew very still and peaceful and Jean's heart did too—and through the silence there came a voice so tender and loving—so gentle that the auntie's eyes were full of tears, and Jean wanted to listen forever, and the voice said, "Jean, inasmuch as ye did it unto one of the least of these, my brethren, ye did it unto ME."

*Adapted from the French of Francois Coppee, by Nannie-Lee-Frayser.

HOW THE FIR TREE BECAME THE CHRISTMAS TREE*

By Aunt Hede, in "Kindergarten Magazine"

This is the story of how the fir tree became the Christmas tree.

At the time when the Christ Child was born all the people, the animals, and the trees, and plants were very happy. The Child was born to bring peace and happiness to the whole world. People came daily to see the little One, and they always brought gifts with them.

There were three trees standing near the crypt which saw the people, and they wished that they, too, might give presents to the Christ Child.

The Palm said: "I will choose my most beautiful leaf, and place it as a fan over the Child."

"And I," said the Olive, "will sprinkle sweet-smelling oil upon His head."

"What can I give to the Child?" asked the Fir, who stood near.

"You!" cried the others. "You have nothing to offer Him. Your needles would prick Him, and your tears are sticky."

So the poor little Fir tree was very unhappy, and it said: "Yes, you are right. I have nothing to offer the Christ Child."

Now, quite near the trees stood the Christmas Angel, who had heard all that the trees had said. The Angel was sorry for the Fir tree who was so lowly and without envy of the other trees. So, when it was dark, and the stars came out, he begged a few of the little stars to come down and rest upon the branches of the Fir tree. They did as the Christmas Angel asked, and the Fir tree shone suddenly with a beautiful light.

And, at that very moment, the Christ Child opened His eyes—for He had been asleep—and as the lovely light fell upon Him He smiled.

Every year people keep the dear Christmas Child's birthday by giving gifts to each other, and every year, in remembrance of His first birthday, the Christmas Angel places in every house a fir tree, also. Covered with starry candles it shines for the children as the stars shone for the Christ Child. The Fir tree was rewarded for its meekness, for to no other tree is it given to shine upon so many happy faces.

*From "For the Children's Hour," by Bailey and Lewis. Used by permission of the authors and also the publishers—Milton Bradley Company.

THE MAGI IN THE WEST AND THEIR SEARCH FOR THE CHRIST*

A Tale for the Christmas-Tide

By Frederick E. Dewhurst

The Mountain of Vision

Now, it happened a long time ago, in the year ——, but the exact year does not matter, because you will not find this story written in the history of any of the nations of the world. But in one of the countries of Europe bordering on the Mediterranean Sea was a lofty mountain, which, to the dwellers in the plains below, seemed to reach to the very sky. At times its summit was covered with clouds, so that it could not be seen; at other times it stood out fair and clear, as though silently asking the people to look up and not down. The lower slopes of the mountain were covered with olive trees, with groves of oranges and lemons, and with vineyards, and they were dotted here and there with the little white cottages of the peasants who made their living from these groves and vineyards, the fruit of which they sold in the city not far away.

Sunset in the Sea

Along the mountain-side wound a foot-trail even to the summit, and nowhere, in all the region, was there a finer view of the Mediterranean than from the summit of this mountain. In the long summer afternoons the peasants and children would climb to the top and look off on the lovely picture of land and sea. Then they would eat their simple lunch of bread and dates and olives

---

and quench their thirst from the spring on the mountain-side, which they called "Dew-of-heaven," so clear and fresh and sparkling was it; and when the sun began to touch the western sky with his pencils of gold and carmine and purple, they hastened down, that they might reach their cottages before the night shut in.

A Stranger Cometh

On the day when this story begins a man was standing on the summit of the mountain looking across the sea in the direction where you will find Tyre and Joppa on the map. He was, very plainly, not one of the peasants who lived on the mountain-side. He looked about sixty years of age; he was tall and erect, though he carried a staff in his hand. His hair and beard were long and flowing, and almost gray, but his eye was clear and penetrating, and he was looking across the sea as though he expected some one to appear.

And while he stood there gazing seaward, there appeared a second man on the summit, helping himself up with his staff, and panting with the effort of the long climb. From his dress and manner it was plain that this man, too, was not one of the peasants, for, like the first comer, he seemed to belong to another age and clime. The two men glanced at each other and gave such greeting as strangers might who should meet in so solitary a spot as a mountain summit. Then both lapsed into silence and looked off across the sea.

And Findeth a Friend

Presently the last comer seemed to awake from his reverie. He walked over to the place where the other man was sitting, still gazing off toward Joppa, and touched him on the shoulder: "A thousand pardons, my friend," he said, "but my mind is haunted with some far-off recollection, as though in some other land and some far-off time I had seen thy face. Wilt thou have the kindness to tell me thy name?"

Without lifting his eyes from the sea, and in a tone which seemed regretful and sad, the stranger replied: "My name is Gaspard."

A Far-off Pilgrimage Recalled

"Gaspard! Indeed, then have I seen thee! Look at me, my friend; dost thou not remember me? My name is Melchoir. Dost thou not recall that time, how long I know not, when thou and I and Balthazar followed a star which led us to a little Jewish hamlet, thou bearing gold and I frankincense, and Balthazar myrrh? Dost thou not remember how, on the long journey thither, we talked about the young Prince, whom we expected to find in a royal palace, and how at last when we reached the village, following the star, we were led not to a palace but to a little inn, and not even to a room within the inn, but to the stable-yard, where we found a sweet-faced woman bending over a babe cradled in a manger; and standing near, a sturdy peasant, proud and happy, whose name was Joseph? Dost thou not remember, too, that when we had recovered from our surprise, we left our gifts and greetings, and went our way as men who had been dreaming? Gaspard, dost thou not remember?"

And Wanderings in Many Lands

And Gaspard, looking now intently in the other's face, replied: "Yes, Melchoir, I remember thee, and I remember the journey of which thou hast spoken better than I remember aught else. Neither have I forgotten the surprise and disappointment with which we came to the place whither the star led us; nor how, after leaving our gifts, we went away as in a dream; and, Melchoir, I have been dreaming ever since. Even here hast thou found me in a dream of perplexity. I am still Gaspard, the wandering magician; for how many years I know not, I have wandered up and down these lands of Europe. I have crossed the seas; in every place I have sought to find the kingdom over which we were told this young prince was one day to reign. Dost thou not remember that we were told His kingdom was to last forever, that He would reign in it himself forever and would never die? Alas! I have lost the old power of the magician's art. I can summon no star to guide me to the place where I shall find this kingdom and its king."

If Only Balthazar Were Here

"Truly, Gaspard," answered Melchoir, "the story of your wanderings is but the repetition of my own; and even now was I drawn to this mountain summit on the self-same errand that brought you here,—to see if I could not discover in the direction of yonder land, where Bethlehem was, some star which might prove to be His star, and which might guide me in the new quest. If only our old companion, Balthazar, were with us now, he might give us the clew to our search, for not only was he more skilful in the magician's art, but he was braver and more courageous, and withal more serene in spirit."

A Song in the Air

Now, even while Melchoir was speaking, a voice was heard a little way down the mountain. Gaspard and Melchoir stopped to listen. The voice was singing, and the words of the song floated up to them distinctly:

If the sun has hid its light, If the day has turned to night, If the heavens are not benign, If the stars refuse to shine—

Heart of man lose not thy hope; Door, there's none that shall not ope; Path, there's none that shall not clear; Heart of man! why shouldst thou fear?

If for years should be thy quest, If for years thou hast no rest, If thou circlest earth and sea, If thou worn and weary be—

Heart of man, lose not thy hope; Door, there's none that shall not ope; Path, there's none that shall not clear; Heart of man! why shouldst thou fear?

Balthazar Cometh

"That," exclaimed Gaspard and Melchoir together, "is the voice of Balthazar." and they hastened to meet him, for he was now almost at the summit, and the refrain of his song was still upon his lips. At that moment Balthazar sprang up from the sloping path into full view of the two men, and, giving each a hand, exclaimed: "Gaspard, Melchoir, beloved companions, I have found you at last.

The peasants below were not mistaken. From their description, I was certain I should find you here. And you, too, have been searching these long years for the kingdom of the Christ! and, like me, you have met with disappointment; but, comrades, be not of faint heart:

Door, there's none that shall not ope; Path, there's none that shall not clear.

Let us hasten down the mountain, for see! the sky is already growing gold and crimson beyond the pillars of Hercules. Let us seek the wayfarer's lodging with the hospitable peasants in the valley, and tomorrow let us begin our search for the Christ anew. We have wandered alone; let us invoke now the star to guide us together."

Forget Not Hospitality

That night, therefore, the three strangers lodged with the simple peasant people in the valley, partaking with thankfulness of the coarse bread, the dates and the red wine—the common fare of their daily life. Nor did they fail to notice a motto inscribed above the fireplace in rude Greek letters:

On the morrow they were ready to begin their search together for the Christ, and they hoped not to wander far before they should find at least the outskirts of His kingdom. But whither should they go? In what direction should they first turn their steps?

Once More a Star

While they were thus wondering and debating, Bathazar suddenly exclaimed: "I see the star!" And behold, a little way before them, and at no great distance above their heads, they discerned in the gray of the early morning a star of pale, opal light, which seemed to move forward as the men moved toward it.

"We must follow the star!" Balthazar said in a whisper. Silently and breathlessly his companions followed on.

Now, so intently did the three men keep their eyes fixed upon the star, and so eagerly did they follow in the direction where it seemed to lead, that it was only after a considerable time they discovered that they had become separated from each other, and that their paths were getting farther and farther apart. Yet, there before each of them was the star, shining with its soft, opalescent light, and still ringing in their ears were the words of Balthazar— "we must follow the star."

The Star Stands Still

So each followed the star, each by himself alone. Gaspard's path wound along near the shore of the gulfs and bays of the Mediterranean, until at last the the star turned southward and drew him nearer and nearer to a great city, and finally stood still over the dome of a vast cathedral. "It must be," thought Gaspard, "that I have come to the end of my search. This must be the capital and palace of the eternal king."

Marbled Aisle's Magnificence

The square in front of the cathedral was thronged with people; multitudes were pouring in through the great portals. Gaspard joined the throngs, and at last found himself under the mighty dome, which seemed to him as far away as the sky itself. Everything in this wonderful place appealed to his imagination. There were great rows of massive columns, symbol of a strength eternal, and they seemed like wide-open arms holding out a welcome to the human race. There were statues and paintings by great masters in art. The light of the sun poured in through many-colored windows, on which were blazoned the deeds of heroes and saints. Strains of music from the great organ in the distance floated out upon the air. Touched and thrilled by all he saw, Gaspard exclaimed to himself: "The place on which I stand is holy ground."

Kyrie Eleison

Soon, however, he perceived that the throngs of people were not lingering, like himself, in awe and wonder over the great columns and the dome, and the statues, and the paintings, and the windows. Their eyes were fixed intently upon something that was going on in the far end of the cathedral. An altar was there, and priests in white robes passing up and down before it, and tall tapers burning around it. Near the altar was the image of a man hanging from a cross; his hands and feet were pierced with nails, and a cruel wound was in his side. The people were gazing at this altar, and at the image, and at what the white-robed priests were doing. The strains of solemn music from the organ blended with the voices of priests chanting the service. Clouds of incense rose from censers, swung with solemn motion by the altar-boys, and the fragrance of the incense was wafted down the long aisles. At last, the tinkling of a bell. The organ became silent for an instant, as though it felt within its heart the awful solemnity of the moment; and then it burst forth into new rapture, and the people began pouring out through the great doors.

We Must Follow the Star

Gaspard went forth with the throng into the cathedral square. "And this," he said, "is the end of my search. I have found the Christ. His kingdom is in the imagination of man. How beautiful, how wonderful, how strange it was! 'Dominus vobiscum,' did not the priests say? Here, then, at last I have found the city of the great King."

But as he lingered, behold! the star which had stood over the dome of the cathedral was now before him, as at first, and seemed to waver and tremble, as if beckoning him on. So, although his feet seemed bound to the spot, and his heart was still throbbing with the deep feelings the cathedral service had created in him, remembering the words of Balthazar, "we must follow the star," he slowly and reluctantly walked on.

The Just Shall Live by Faith

In the meantime Melchoir also had followed faithfully the path along which the star seemed to lead. Through forests in which he almost lost his way, across rivers difficult and dangerous to ford—still he followed on. At length Melchoir's star seemed to tarry over the spire of a gothic church, into which the people were going in throngs. Waiting a moment, to be sure that the star was actually standing still, Melchoir went in with the rest. In this place was no altar, such as Gaspard saw; no image on the cross; no white-robed priests; no swinging censers. But, as Melchoir entered he heard strains from the organ, and a chorus of voices was singing an anthem beginning with the words, "Te Deum Laudamus." And when the anthem came to a close, a man clothed in a black robe, such as scholars were wont to wear, rose in his place upon a platform elevated above the people, and began to speak to them about the kingdom of Christ. Melchoir listened in eager expectancy. The Truth Shall Make You Free"The kingdom of the Christ," the preacher said, "is the kingdom of the truth, and the truth is to be continued and kept alive by the strength of man's belief. Those things which have been handed down by holy men and sacred oracles since Christ was here upon the earth, are the truths by which we live. How can Christ live except He live in our beliefs? Why did the Father of all intrust us with our reasons, unless it were that we should make them the instruments of our faith and our salvation? Let us therefore stand in our places, while we recite together the articles of our holy faith."

These and many such words did the scholar-preacher declare. And as he sat there with the people, Melchoir felt the weight of the solemn and earnest words, and he said: "So at last have I come to the end of my search. The kingdom of Christ is in the mind of man. His kingdom is the kingdom of the truth."

More Light Shall Break Forth

Then he followed the throngs as they went forth from the church; but the star which had tarried over the lofty spire was now before him, and the opal light wavered and trembled, as if beckoning him on; and the words of the preacher, "we must believe," seemed to blend with the words of Balthazar, "we must follow the star." So, reluctantly and slowly he followed on.

Thy Sacramental Liturgies

But Balthazar—whither went he, following the star? Over many a rugged way, through many a tangled thicket, through valleys and over hills. His star tarried over no cathedrals; it lingered over no Gothic spires. It seemed capricious and restless and tireless. At times it seemed intent on coming to a pause over the head of some human being, but perhaps it was because these human beings themselves were so restless and so busy that the star could not accomplish its intent. For Balthazar saw these men and women hurrying hither and thither on errands of mercy, or deeds of justice; he saw them ferreting out great wrongs, laying heavy blows on the backs of men who oppressed and defrauded their fellow men.

At length Balthazar seemed to understand the movements of the star, and, drawing nearer, he would seem to hear these men repeating cheering and encouraging words to one another. "Pure religion and undefiled," he heard one exclaiming, "is to visit the fatherless and widows in their affliction, and to keep himself unspotted from the world." And another echoed, "Inasmuch as we do it to the least of these, we do it unto Christ."

The Joy of Doing Good

"Ah! thought Balthazar as he listened, I see the meaning of it now; I am coming to the end of my search. The kingdom of Christ—I have found it. It is in the deeds of men; it is in the conscience and the serving will. Devotion to right, this is the law of the kingdom of Christ."

Then Balthazar turned to go in search of his comrades again; but behold! the opal star was trembling, as if beckoning him on. So, still doubting if he had reached the end of his search, he followed the star.

The Paths Converge

Thus Gaspard, Melchoir and Balthazar, each following the star, at last approached each other. The star of each seemed to melt and blend into the star of the others, and the opal light stood at last in the center of the group. Gaspard exclaimed: "I have found that which we all were seeking. The kingdom of Christ is in the imagination; Christ lives in what man feels."

"Nay," said Melchoir, "I have followed the star, and I have found what we sought. The kingdom of Christ is in the reason of man. Christ lives in what man believes."

"But," cried Balthazar, "my star has led me to a different end. The kingdom of Christ is in the will of man. Christ lives in what man does."

"The truth," once more exclaimed Melchoir, "is the law of the kingdom."

"Not truth," declared Balthazar, "but justice, righteousness, goodness and purity—these are its laws and its marks."

"Nay, comrades beloved, hearken to me," answered Gaspard, "it is the miracle of the divine presence. It is God among men, realized in the holy mass. I beheld it all in yonder cathedral."

But lo! once more the star began to tremble and to change its place.

"Let us follow the star!" Balthazar whispered. "We will follow it," echoed the other two.

Once More the Quest

Then the star led them on, and they followed together until they came at length to the doorway of a little cottage; and within the cottage they saw a woman bending over a cradle, and in the cradle a little child lay sleeping. She was a peasant woman; her clothing was not rich; the furnishing of the cottage was humble and scanty. The cradle itself was rude, as if put together by hands unskilful in tasks like that. But when the mother looked at her babe a sweet smile played about her lips, and a light was in her eyes. Then all suddenly the three men remembered another scene long before, when they were bearers of gold and frankincense and myrrh to another babe.

He That Loveth Knoweth God

And while they stood and wondered by the door, there came a strong and sturdy peasant, broad-shouldered, roughly clad, his face browned in the sun, his hands hardened with toil. He came and stood beside the woman, and they bent together over the cradle of the sleeping child, and the man drew the woman tenderly toward him and kissed her brow.

And still the three men lingered; for behold! the star stood still above the child, and they dared not speak. But the heart of Gaspard was saying in silence, "There is something greater than the repeated miracle of the mass."

And Melchoir was thinking, "There is something mightier even than the mind; something superior to naked truth."

For God Is Love

And Balthazar was confessing to himself that he had found something more potent even than the righteous deed. For here they all beheld how life was made sweet and blessed and holy by the power of love; and by love for a little child, in whom was all weakness and helplessness, whose only voice was a cry, but who was all strong and mighty with the power of God, because he could transform roughness into tenderness, and selfishness into loving care, and poverty itself into gifts of gold and fragrant myrrh.

"Truly, my comrades," Balthazar said, "love is the greatest of all."

"And now I understand," said Gaspard, "how the weak things of the world can confound the mighty."

"And I," added Melchoir, "see what it means for God to come to earth in the form of a little child."

And so they turned away, and the radiance of the star was round about them, and they were saying to each other: "Our search at last is ended."

*Reprinted with the permission of "The Sketching Club," Indianapolis, Ind.

LITTLE GRETCHEN AND THE WOODEN SHOE*

By Elizabeth Harrison

Once upon a time, a long time ago, far away across the great ocean, in a country called Germany, there could be seen a small log hut on the edge of a great forest, whose fir trees extended for miles and miles to the north. This little house, made of heavy hewn logs, had but one room in it. A rough pine door gave entrance to this room, and a small square window admitted the light. At the back of the house was built an old-fashioned stone chimney, out of which in winter curled a thin, blue smoke, showing that there was not very much fire within.

Small as the house was, it was large enough for two people who lived in it. I want to tell you a story today about these two people. One was an old gray-haired woman, so old that the little children of the village, nearly half a mile away, often wondered whether she had come into the world with the huge mountains and the giant fir trees, which stood like giants back of her small hut. Her face was wrinkled all over with deep lines, which, if the children could only have read aright, would have told them of many years of cheerful, happy, self-sacrifice; of loving, anxious, watching beside sick-beds; of quiet endurance of pain, of many a day of hunger and cold, and of a thousand deeds of unselfish love for other people; but, of course, they could not read this strange handwriting. They only knew that she was old and wrinkled, and that she stooped as she walked. None of them seemed to fear her, for her smile was always cheerful, and she had a kindly word for each of them if they chanced to meet her on her way to and from the village. With this old, old woman lived a very little girl. So bright and happy was she that the travellers who passed by the lonesome little house on the edge of the forest often thought of a sunbeam as they saw her. These two people were known in the village as Granny Goodyear and Little Gretchen.

The winter had come and the frost had snapped off many of the smaller branches of the pine trees in the forest. Gretchen and her granny were up by daybreak each morning. After their simple breakfast of oatmeal, Gretchen would run to the little closet and fetch Granny's old woolen shawl, which seemed almost as old as Granny herself. Gretchen always claimed the right to put the shawl over Granny's head, even though she had to climb onto the wooden bench to do it. After carefully pinning it under Granny's chin, she gave her a good-bye kiss, and Granny started out for her morning's work in the forest. This work was nothing more nor less than the gathering up of the twigs and branches which the autumn winds and winter frosts had thrown upon the ground. These were carefully gathered into a large bundle which Granny tied together with a strong linen band. She then managed to lift the bundle to her shoulder and trudged off to the village with it. Here she sold the fagots for kindling wood to the people of the village. Sometimes she would get only a few pence each day, and sometimes a dozen or more, but on this money little Gretchen and she managed to live; they had their home, and the forest kindly furnished the wood for the fire which kept them warm in winter.

In the summer time Granny had a little garden at the back of the house, where she raised, with little Gretchen's help, a few potatoes and turnips and onions. These she carefully stored away for winter use. To this meagre supply, the pennies, gained by selling the twigs from the forest, added the oatmeal for Gretchen and a little black coffee for Granny. Meat was a thing they never thought of having. It cost too much money. Still, Granny and Gretchen were very happy, because they loved each other dearly. Sometimes Gretchen would be left alone all day long in the hut, because Granny would have some work to do in the village after selling her bundle of sticks and twigs. It was during these long days that little Gretchen had taught herself to sing the song which the wind sang to the pine branches. In the summer time she learned the chirp and twitter of the birds, until her voice might almost be mistaken for a bird's voice, she learned to dance as the swaying shadows did, and even to talk to the stars which shone through the little square window when Granny came home late or too tired to talk.

Sometimes, when the weather was fine, or her Granny had an extra bundle of knitted stockings to take to the village, she would let little Gretchen go along with her. It chanced that one of these trips to the town came just the week before Christmas, and Gretchen's eyes were delighted by the sight of the lovely Christmas trees which stood in the window of the village store. It seemed to her that she would never tire of looking at the knit dolls, the woolly lambs, the little wooden shops with their queer, painted men and women in them, and all the other fine things. She had never owned a plaything in her whole life; therefore, toys which you and I would not think much of seemed to her very beautiful.

That night, after their supper of baked potatoes was over, and little Gretchen had cleared away the dishes and swept up the hearth, because Granny dear was so tired, she brought her own little wooden stool and placed it very near Granny's feet and sat down upon it. folding her hands on her lap. Granny knew that this meant that she wanted to be told about something, so she smilingly laid away the large Bible which she had been reading. and took up her knitting, which was as much as to say: "Well. Gretchen, dear, Granny is ready to listen."

"Granny," said Gretchen slowly, "It's almost Christmas time, isn't it?"

"Yes, dearie," said Granny, "only five days more now," and then she sighed, but little Gretchen was so happy that she did not notice Granny's sigh.

"What do you think, Granny, I'll get this Christmas?" said she, looking up eagerly into Granny's face.

"Ah, child, child," said Granny, shaking her head, "you'll have no Christmas this year. We are too poor for that."

"Oh, but Granny," interrupted little Gretchen, "think of all the beautiful toys we saw in the village today. Surely Santa Claus has sent enough for every little child."

"Ah, dearie, those toys are for people who can pay for them, and we have no money to spend for Christmas toys."

"Well, Granny," said Gretchen, "perhaps some of the little children who live in the great house on the hill at the other end of the village, will be willing to share some of their toys with me. They will be glad to give some to a little girl who has none."

"Dear child, dear child," said Granny, leaning forward and stroking the soft, shiny hair of the little girl, "your heart is full of love. You would be glad to bring a Christmas to every child; but their heads are so full of what they are going to get that they forget all about anybody else but themselves." Then she sighed and shook her head.

"Well, Granny," said Gretchen, her bright, happy tone of voice growing a little less joyous, "perhaps the dear Santa Claus will show some of the village children how to make presents that do not cost money, and some of them may surprise me Christmas morning with a present. And, Granny, dear," added she, springing up from her low stool, "can't I gather some of the pine branches and take them to the old sick man who lives in the house by the mill, so that he can have the sweet smell of our forest in his room all Christmas day?"

"Yes, dearie," said Granny, "you may do what you can to make the Christmas bright and happy, but you must not expect any present yourself."

"Oh, but, Granny," said little Gretchen, her face brightening, "you forgot all about the shining Christmas angels, who came down to earth and sang their wonderful song the night the beautiful Christ-Child was born! They are so loving and good that they will not forget any little child. I shall ask my dear stars tonight to tell them of us. You know," she added, with a look of relief, "the stars are so very high that they must know the angels quite well as they come and go with their messages from the loving God."

Granny sighed as she half whispered. "Poor child, poor child!" but Gretchen threw her arm around Granny's neck and gave her a hearty kiss, saying as she did so: "Oh, Granny, Granny, you don't talk to the stars often enough, else you would not be sad at Christmas time." Then she danced all around the room, whirling her little skirts about her to show Granny how the wind had made the snow dance that day. She looked so droll and funny that Granny forgot her cares and worries and laughed with little Gretchen over her new snow dance. The days passed on and the morning before Christmas Eve came. Gretchen having tidied up the little room—for Granny had taught her to be a careful little housewife—was off to the forest, singing a birdlike song, almost as happy and free as the birds themselves. She was very busy that day preparing a surprise for Granny. First, however, she gathered the most beautiful of the fir branches within her reach to take the next morning to the old sick man who lived by the mill.

The day was all too short for the happy little girl. When Granny came trudging wearily home that night, she found the frame of the doorway covered with green pine branches.

"It is to welcome you, Granny! It is to welcome you!" cried Gretchen; "our dear old home wanted to give you a Christmas welcome. Don't you see, the branches of the evergreen make it look as if it were smiling all over, and it is trying to say, 'A happy Christmas to you Granny'."

Granny laughed and kissed the little girl, as they opened the door and went in together. Here was a new surprise for Granny. The four posts of the wooden bed, which stood in one corner of the room, had been trimmed by the busy little fingers, with smaller and more flexible branches of the pine trees. A small bouquet of red mountain ash berries stood at each side of the fireplace, and these, together with the trimmed posts of the bed, gave the plain old room quite a festive look. Gretchen laughed and clapped her hands and danced about until the house seemed full of music to poor, tired Granny, whose heart had been sad as she turned toward their home that night, thinking of the disappointment that must come to loving little Gretchen the next morning.

After supper was over little Gretchen drew her stool up to Granny's side, and laying her soft, little hands on Granny's knee asked to be told once again the story of the coming of the Christ-Child; how the night that he was born the beautiful angels had sung their wonderful song, and how the whole sky had become bright with a strange and glorious light, never seen by the people of earth before. Gretchen had heard the story many, many times before, but she never grew tired of it, and now that Christmas Eve had come again, the happy little child wanted to hear it once more.

When Granny had finished telling it the two sat quiet and silent for a little while thinking it over; then Granny rose and said that it was time for her to go to bed. She slowly took off her heavy wooden shoes, such as are worn in that country, and placed them beside the hearth.Gretchen looked thoughtfully at them for a minute or two, and then she said, "Granny, don't you think that *somebody* in all this wide world will think of us tonight?"

"Nay, Gretchen, I do not think any one will."

"Well, then, Granny," said Gretchen, "the Christmas angels will, I know; so I am going to take one of your wooden shoes and put it on the windowsill outside, so that they may see it as they pass by. I am sure the stars will tell the Christmas angels where the shoe is."

"Ah, you foolish, foolish child," said Granny, "you are only getting ready for a disappointment. Tomorrow morning there will be nothing whatever in the shoe. I can tell you that now."

But little Gretchen would not listen. She only shook her head and cried out: "Ah, Granny, you do not talk enough to the stars." With this she seized the shoe, and opening the door, hurried out to place it on the window sill. It was very dark without and something soft and cold seemed to gently kiss her hair and face. Gretchen knew by this that it was snowing, and she looked up to the sky, anxious to see if the stars were in sight, but a strong wind was tumbling the dark, heavy snow-clouds about and had shut away all else.

"Never mind," said Gretchen softly to herself, "the stars are up there, even if I can't see them, and the Christmas angels do not mind snow storms."

Just then a rough wind went sweeping by the little girl, whispering something to her which she could not understand, and then it made a sudden rush up to the snow clouds and parted them, so that the deep mysterious sky appeared beyond, and shining down out of the midst of it was Gretchen's favorite star.

"Ah, little star, little star!" said the child, laughing aloud, "I knew you were there, though I could not see you. Will you whisper to the Christmas angels as they come by that little Gretchen wants so very much to have a Christmas gift tomorrow morning, if they have one to spare, and that she has put one of Granny's shoes upon the windowsill for it?"

A moment more and the little girl, standing on tiptoe had reached the windowsill and placed the shoe upon it, and was back again in the house beside Granny and the warm fire.

The two went quietly to bed, and that night as little Gretchen knelt to pray to the Heavenly Father, she thanked him for having sent the Christ-Child into the world to teach all mankind to be loving and unselfish, and in a few minutes she was sleeping, dreaming of the Christmas angels.

The next morning, very early, even before the sun was up, little Gretchen was awakened by the sound of sweet music coming from the village. She listened for a moment and then she knew that the choir boys were singing the Christmas carols in the open air of the village street. She sprang up out of bed and began to dress herself as quickly as possible, singing as she dressed. While Granny was slowly putting on her clothes, little Gretchen having finished dressing herself, unfastened the door and hurried out to see what the Christmas angels had left in the old wooden shoe.

The white snow covered everything—trees, stumps, roads, and pastures—until the whole world looked like fairy land. Gretchen climbed up on a large stone which was beneath the window and carefully lifted down the wooden shoe. The snow tumbled off of it in a shower over the little girl's hands, but she did not heed that;

she ran hurriedly back into the house, putting her hand into the toe of the shoe as she ran.

"Oh, Granny, Granny!" she exclaimed; "you did not believe the Christmas angels would think about us, but see, they have, they have! Here is a dear little bird nestled down in the toe of your shoe Oh, isn't he beautiful?"

Granny came forward and looked at what the child was holding lovingly in her hand. There she saw a tiny chick-a-dee, whose wing was evidently broken by the rough and boisterous winds of the night before, and who had taken shelter in the safe, dry toe of the old wooden shoe. She gently took the little bird out of Gretchen's hands, and skilfully bound his broken wing to his side, so that he need not hurt himself trying to fly with it. Then she showed Gretchen how to make a nice warm nest for the little stranger, close beside the fire and when their breakfast was ready, she let Gretchen feed the little bird with a few moist crumbs.

Later in the day Gretchen carried the fresh, green boughs to the old sick man by the mill, and on her way home stopped to enjoy the Christmas toys of some other children that she knew, never once wishing they were hers. When she reached home she found that the little bird had gone to sleep. Soon, however, he opened his eyes and stretched his head up, saying just as plain as a bird can say:

"Now, my new friends, I want you to give me something more to eat." Gretchen gladly fed him again, and then, holding him in her lap, she softly and gently stroked his gray feathers until the little creature seemed to lose all fear of her. That evening Granny taught her a Christmas hymn and told her another beautiful Christmas story. Then Gretchen made up a funny little story to tell the birdie. He winked his eyes and turned his head from side to side in such a droll fashion that Gretchen laughed until the tears came.

As Granny and she got ready for bed that night, Gretchen put her arms softly around Granny's neck, and whispered: "What a beautiful Christmas we have had today, Granny. Is there anything more lovely in all the world than Christmas?"

"Nay, child, nay," said Granny, "not to such loving hearts as yours."

*Reprinted by permission of the author from her collection, "Christmastide." Published by the Chicago Kindergarten College.

THE LITTLE SHEPHERD*

By Maud Lindsay

The shepherd was sick and the shepherd's wife looked out from her door with anxious eyes. "Who will carry the sheep to the pasture lands today?" she said to her little boy Jean.

"I will," cried Jean, "I will. Mother, let me."

Jean and his father and mother lived long ago in a sunny land across the sea, where flowers bloom, and birds sing, and shepherds feed their flocks in the green valleys. Every morning, as soon as it was light, Jean's father was up and away with his sheep. He had never missed a morning before, and the sheep were bleating in the fold as if to say, "Don't forget us today."

The sheep were Jean's playfellows. There was nothing he liked better than to wander with them in the pleasant pastures, and already they knew his voice and followed at his call.

"Let the lad go," said his old grandfather. "When I was no older than he I watched my father's flock."

Jean's father said the same thing, so the mother made haste to get the little boy ready.

"Eat your dinner when the shadows lie straight across the grass," she said as she kissed him good-bye.

"And keep the sheep from the forest paths," called his sick father.

"And watch, for it is when the shepherd is not watching that the wolf comes to the flock," said the old grandfather.

"Never fear," said little Jean. "The wolf shall not have any of my white lambs."

They were white sheep and black sheep and frolicsome lambs in the shepherd's flock, and each one had a name of its own. There was Babbette, and Nannette, and Pierrot, and Jeannot,—I cannot tell them all, but Jean knew every name.

"Come, Bettine and Marie. Come, Pierrot and Croisette. Come, pretty ones all," he called as he led them from the fold that day. "I will carry you to the meadows where the daisies grow."

"Baa," answered the sheep, well satisfied, as they followed him down the king's highway, and over the hill to the pasture lands.

The other shepherds were already there with their flocks, so Jean was not lonely. He watered his sheep at the dancing brook that ran through the flowers, and led them along its shady banks to feed in the sunny fields beyond, and not one lambkin strayed from his care to the forest paths.

The forest lay dim and shadowy on one side of the pasture lands. The deer lived there, and the boars that fed upon acorns, and many other creatures that loved the wild woods. There had been wolves in the forest, but the king's knights had driven them away and the shepherds feared them no longer. Only the old men like Jean's grandfather, and the little boys like Jean, talked of them still.

Jean was not afraid. Oh, no. There was not a lamb in the flock so merry and fearless as he. He sang with the birds and ran with the brook, and laughed till the echoes laughed with him as he watched the sheep from early morn to noon, when the shadows fell straight across the grass and it was time for him to eat his dinner.

There were little cakes in Jean's dinner basket. He had seen his mother put them there, but he had not tasted a single one when, out on the king's highway, beyond the hill, he heard the sound of pipes and drums, and the tramp, tramp of many feet.

The other shepherds heard too, and they began to listen and to stare and to run. "The king and his knights are coming," they cried. "Come let us see them as they pass by."

"Who will take care of the sheep?" asked Jean, but nobody answered, so he too left his dinner and ran with the rest, away from the pastures and up the hillside path that led to the highway.

"How pleased my mother will be when I tell her that I have seen the king," he said to himself, and he was hurrying over the hill top when all at once he remembered the forest, and the wolf, and his grandfather's words.

"Come on," called the others.

"I must stay with the sheep," answered he; and he turned and went back, though the pipes and the drums all seemed to say, "Come this way, come this way." He could scarcely keep from crying as he listened.

There was nothing in sight to harm the sheep, and the pasture lands were quiet and peaceful, but into the forest that very day a hungry gray wolf had come. His eyes were bright and his ears were sharp and his four feet were as soft as velvet, as he came creeping, creeping, creeping under the houses and through the tanglewood. He put his nose out and sniffed the air, and he put his head out and spied the sheep left alone in the meadows. "Now's my chance," he said, and out he sprang just as little Jean down the hill.

"Wolf, wolf, wolf!" shouted Jean. "Wolf, wolf, wolf!" He was only a little boy, but he was brave and his voice rang clear as a bugle call over the valley, and over the hill, "Wolf, wolf, wolf!"

The shepherds and knights and the king himself came running and riding to answer his cry, and as for the gray wolf, he did not even stop to look behind him as he sped away to the forest shades. He ran so fast and he ran so far that he was never seen in the king's country again, though the shepherds in the pastures watched for him day after day.

Jean led his flock home at eventide, white sheep and black sheep and frolicsome lambs, not one was missing.

"Was the day long?" asked his mother, who was watching in the doorway for him.

"Are the sheep all in?" called the sick father.

"Did the wolf come?" said the old grandfather; but there is no need for me to tell you what Jean said. You can imagine that for yourself.

*From "More Mother Stories," by Maud Lindsay. Used by permission of the author and the publishers—the Milton Bradley Company.

BABOUSCKA*

Russian Legend

It was the night the dear Christ Child came to Bethlehem. In a country far away from Him, an old, old woman named Babouscka sat in her snug little house by her warm fire. The wind was drifting the snow outside and howling down the chimney, but it only made Babouscka's fire burn more brightly.

"How glad I am that I may stay indoors!" said Babouscka, holding her hands out to the bright blaze. But suddenly she heard a loud rap at her door. She opened it and her candle shone on three old men standing outside in the snow. Their beards were as white as the snow, and so long that they reached the ground. Their eyes shone kindly in the light of Babouscka's candle, and their arms were full of precious things—boxes of jewels, and sweet-smelling oils, and ointments.

"We have traveled far, Babouscka," said they, "and we stop to tell you of the Baby Prince born this night in Bethlehem. He comes to rule the world and teach all men to be loving and true. We carry Him gifts. Come with us, Babouscka!"

But Babouscka looked at the driving snow, and then inside at her cozy room and the crackling fire. "It is too late for me to go with you, good sirs," she said, "the weather is too cold." She went inside again and shut the door, and the old men journeyed on to Bethlehem without her. But as Babouscka sat by her fire, rocking, she began to think about the little Christ Child, for she loved all babies.

"Tomorrow I will go to find Him," she said; "tomorrow, when it is light, and I will carry Him some toys."

So when it was morning Babouscka put on her long cloak, and took her staff, and filled a basket with the pretty things a baby would like—gold balls, and wooden toys, and strings of silver cobwebs—and she set out to find the Christ Child.

But, oh! Babouscka had forgotten to ask the three old men the road to Bethlehem, and they had traveled so far through the night that she could not overtake them. Up and down the roads she hurried, through woods and fields and towns, saying to whomsoever she met: "I go to find the Christ Child. Where does he lie? I bring some pretty toys for His sake."

But no one could tell her the way to go, and they all said: "Farther on, Babouscka, farther on." So she traveled on, and on, and on for years and years—but she never found the little Christ Child.

They say that old Babouscka is traveling still, looking for Him. When it comes Christmas eve, and the children are lying fast asleep, Babouscka comes softly through the snowy fields and towns, wrapped in her long cloak and carrying her basket on her arm. With her staff she raps gently at the doors and goes inside and holds her candle close to the little children's faces.

"Is He here?" she asks. "Is the little Christ Child here?" And then she turns sorrowfully away again, crying: "Farther on, farther on." But before she leaves she takes a toy from her basket and lays it beside the pillow for a Christmas gift. "For His sake," she says softly and then hurries on through the years and forever in search of the little Christ Child.

*From "For the Children's Hour," by Bailey and Lewis. Used by permission of the authors and also the publishers—Milton Bradley Company.

THE BOY WITH THE BOX

By Mary Griggs Van Voorhis

It was an ideal Christmas day. The sun shone brightly but the air was crisp and cold, and snow and ice lay sparkling everywhere. A light wind, the night before, had swept the blue, icebound river clean of scattering snow; and, by two o'clock in the afternoon, the broad bend near Creighton's mill was fairly alive with skaters. The girls in gay caps and scarfs, the boys in sweaters and mackinaws of every conceivable hue, with here and there a plump, matronly figure in a plush coat or a tiny fellow in scarlet, made a picture of life and brilliancy worthy of an artist's finest skill.

Tom Reynolds moved in and out among the happy throng, with swift, easy strokes, his cap on the back of his curly head, and his brown eyes shining with excitement. Now and again, he glanced down with pardonable pride, at the brand new skates that twinkled beneath his feet. "Jolly Ramblers," sure enough "Jolly Ramblers" they were! Ever since Ralph Evans had remarked, with a tantalizing toss of his handsome head, that "no game fellow would try to skate on anything but 'Jolly Ramblers,'" Tom had yearned, with an inexpressible longing, for a pair of these wonderful skates. And now they were his and the ice was fine and the Christmas sun was shining!

Tom was rounding the big bend for the fiftieth time, when he saw, skimming gracefully toward him through the merry crowd, a tall boy in a fur-trimmed coat, his handsome head proudly erect.

"That's Ralph Evans now," said Tom to himself. "Just wait till you see these skates, old boy, and maybe you won't feel so smart!" And with slow, cautious strokes, he made his way through laughing boys and girls to a place just in front of the tall skater, coming toward him down the broad white way. When Ralph was almost upon him, Tom paused and in conspicuous silence, looked down at his shining skates.

"Hullo," said Ralph good naturedly, seizing Tom's arm and swinging around. Then, taking in the situation with a careless glance, he added, "Get a new pair of skates for Christmas?"

"'Jolly Ramblers,'" said Tom impressively, "the best 'Jolly Ramblers' in the market!"

Ralph was a full half head the taller, but, as Tom delivered himself of this speech with his head held high, he felt every inch as tall as the boy before him.

If Ralph was deeply impressed he failed to show it, as he answered carelessly, "Huh, that so? Pretty good little skates they are, the 'Jolly Ramblers!'"

"You said no game fellow would use any other make," said Tom hotly.

"O but that was nearly a year ago," said Ralph. "I got a new pair of skates for Christmas, too," he added, as if it had just occurred to him, "'Club House' skates, something new in the market just this season. Just look at the curve of that skate, will you?" he added, lifting a foot for inspection, "and that clamp that you couldn't shake off if you had to! They're guaranteed for a year, too, and if anything gives out, you get a new pair for nothing. Three and a half, they cost, at Mr. Harrison's hardware store. I gave my 'Jolly Ramblers' to a kid about your size. A mighty good little skate they are!" And, with a long, graceful stroke, Ralph Evans skated away.

And it seemed to Tom Reynolds that all his Christmas joy went skimming away behind him. The sun still shone, the ice still gleamed, the skaters laughed and sang, but Tom moved slowly on, with listless, heavy strokes. The "Jolly Ramblers" still twinkled beneath his feet, but he looked down at them no more. What was the use of "Jolly Ramblers" when Ralph Evans had a pair of "Club House" skates that cost a dollar more, had a graceful curve, and a faultless clamp, and were guaranteed for a year?

It was only four o'clock when Tom slipped his new skates carelessly over his shoulder and started up the bank for home. He was slouching down the main street, head down, hands thrust deep into his pockets, when, on turning a corner, he ran plump into—a full moon! Now I know it is rather unusual for full moons to be walking about the streets by daylight; but that is the only adequate description of the round, freckled face that beamed at Tom from behind a great box, held by two sturdy arms.

"That came pretty near being a collision," said the owner of the full moon, still beaming, as he set down the box and leaned against a building to rest a moment.

"Nobody hurt, I guess," said Tom.

"Been down to the ice?" asked the boy, eagerly. "I could see the skaters from Patton's store. O, I see, you got some new skates for Christmas! Ain't they beauties, now?" And he beamed on the despised "Jolly Ramblers" with his heart in his little blue eyes.

"A pretty good little pair of skates," said Tom, in Ralph's condescending tone.

"Good! Well I should guess yes! And Christmas ice just made o' purpose!" In spite of his ill humor, Tom could not help responding to the warm interest of the shabby boy at his side. He knew him to be Harvey McGinnis, the son of a poor Irish widow, who worked at Patton's department store out of school hours. Looking at the great box with an awakening interest, he remarked, kindly, "What you been doin' with yourself on Christmas day?"

"Want to know, sure enough?" said Harvey, mysteriously, his round face beaming more brightly than ever, "Well, I've been doin' the Santy Claus act down at Patton's store.

"About a week ago," he went on, leaning back easily against the tall building and thrusting his hands down deep into his well worn pockets, "about a week ago, as I was cleaning out the storeroom, I came on three big boxes with broken dolls in 'em. Beauties they were, I kin tell you, the Lady Jane in a blue silk dress, the Lady Clarabel in pink, and the Lady Matilda in shimmerin' white. Nothin' wrong with 'em either only broken rubbers that put their jints out o' whack and set their heads arollin' this way and that. 'They could be fixed in no time, I ses to myself, 'and what a prize they'd be fer the kids to be sure!' For mom and me had racked our brains considerable how we'd scrape together the money for Christmas things for the girls.

"So I went to the boss and I asked him right out what he'd charge me for the three ladies just as they wus, and he ses, 'Jimmie,' he ses (I've told him me name a dozen times, but he allus calls me 'Jimmie'), 'Jimmie,' he ses, 'if you'll come down on Christmas day and help me take down the fixin's and fix up the store for regular trade, I'll give you the dolls fer nothin',' he ses.

"So I explained to the kids that Santy'd be late to our house this year (with so many to see after it wouldn't be strange) and went down to the store early this morning and finished me work and fixed up the ladies es good es new. Would you like to be seein' 'em, now?" he added, turning to the great box with a look of pride.

"Sure, I'd like to see 'em," said Tom.

With careful, almost reverent touch, Harvey untied the string and opened the large box, disclosing three smaller boxes, one above the other. Opening the first box, he revealed a really handsome doll in a blue silk dress, with large dark eyes that opened and shut and dark, curling locks of "real hair."

"This is the Lady Jane," he said, smoothing her gay frock with gentle fingers. "We're goin' to give her to Kitty. Kitty's hair is pretty and curly, but she hates it, 'cause it's red; and she thinks black hair is the prettiest kind in the world. Ain't it funny how all of us will be wantin' what we don't have ourselves?"

Tom did not reply to this bit of philosophy; but he laid a repentant hand on the "Jolly Ramblers" as if he knew he had wronged them in his heart. "That's as handsome a doll as ever I saw and no mistake," he said.

Pleased with this praise, Harvey opened the second box and disclosed the Lady Matilda with fair golden curls and a dress of "shimmerin' white." "The LadyMatilda goes to Josephine," said Harvey. "Josephine has black hair, straight as a string, and won't she laugh, though, to see them fetchin' yellow curls?"

"She surely ought to be glad," said Tom.

The Lady Clarabel was another fair-haired lady in a gown of the brightest pink. "This here beauty's for the baby," said Harvey, his eyes glowing. "She don't care if the hair's black or yellow, but won't that stunnin' dress make her eyes pop out?"

"They'll surely believe in Santy when they see those beauties," said Tom.

'That's just what I was sayin' to mom this morning," said Harvey. "Kitty's had some doubts, (she's almost nine), but when she sees those fine ladies she'll be dead sure mom and I didn't buy 'em. If I had a Santy Claus suit, I'd dress up and hand 'em out myself."

Tom's face lighted with a bright idea. "My brother Bob's got a Santa Claus suit that he used in a show last Christmas," he said. "Say, let me dress up and play Santa. for you. The girls would never guess who I was!"

"Wouldn't they stare, though!" said Harvey, delightedly. "But do you think you'd want to take time," he asked apologetically, "and you with a new pair of skates and the ice like this?"

"Of course, I want to if you'll let me," said Tom. "I'll skate down the river and meet you anywhere you say."

"Out in our back yard, then, at seven o'clock," said Harvey.

"All right, I'll be there!" and with head up, and skates clinking, Tom hurried away.

It was a flushed, excited boy who burst into the Reynolds' quiet sitting room a few minutes later, with his skates still hanging on his shoulder and his cap in his hand. "Say, mother," he cried, "can I have Bob's Santa Claus suit this evening, please? I'm going to play Santa Claus for Harvey McGinnis!"

"Play Santa Claus for Harvey McGinnis. What do you mean, child?"

"You know Mrs. McGinnis, mother, that poor woman who lives in the little house by the river. Her husband got killed on the railroad last winter, you know. Well, Harvey, her boy, has fixed up some grand looking dolls for his sisters and he wants me to come out and play Santa tonight," and Tom launched out into a long story about Harvey and his good fortune.

"He must be a splendid boy," said Mrs. Reynolds, heartily, "and I am sure I shall be glad to have you go."

"And another thing, mother," said Tom, hesitating a little, "do you think grandma would care if I spent part of that five dollars she gave me for a pair of skates for Harvey? He hasn't any skates at all, and I know he'd just love to have some!"

"It is generous of you to think of it," said his mother, much pleased, "and you would still have two and a half for that little trip down to grandma's."

"But I'd like to get him some 'Club House' skates," said Tom. "They're a new kind that cost three dollars and a half."

"But I thought you said the 'Jolly Ramblers' were the best skates made?" Mrs. Reynolds looked somewhat hurt as she glanced from Tom to the skates on his shoulder and back to Tom again.

"They are, mother, they're just dandies!" said Tom blushing with shame that he could ever have despised his mother's gift. "But these 'Club House' skates are just the kind for Harvey. You see, Harvey's shoes are old and worn, and these 'Club House' skates have clamps that you can't shake loose if you have to. Then, if anything happens to them before the year's up, you get a new pair free; and Harvey, you know, wouldn't have any money to be fixing skates."

"Well, do as you like," said Mrs. Reynolds, pleased with Tom's eagerness, for such a spell of generosity was something new in her selfish younger son. "But remember, you will have to wait a while for your visit to grandma."

"All right, and thank you, mother," said Tom. "You can buy the skates down at Harrison's and I'm going over and ask Mr. Harrison if he won't open up the store and get a pair for me for a special time like this. I'm most sure he will!" and away he flew.

That evening, at seven, as the moon was rising over the eastern hills, a short, portly Santa Claus stepped out of the dry reeds by the river bank and walked with wonderfully nimble feet, right into the McGinnis' little back yard. As he neared the small back porch, a dark figure rose to greet him, one hand held up in warning, the other holding at arm's length, a bulky grain sack, full to the brim.

"Here's yer pack, Santy," he whispered, gleefully. "They're all waitin' in the front room yonder. I'll slip in the back way, whilst you go round and give a good thump at the front door and mom'll let you in."

Trembling with eagerness, Tom tiptoed round the house, managing to slip an oblong package into the capacious depths of the big sack as he did so. Thump, thump! how his knock reëchoed in the frosty air! The door swung wide, and Mrs. McGinnis' gaunt figure stood before him.

"Good evenin', Santy, come right in," she said.

Tom had always thought what a homely woman Harvey's mother was when he happened to meet her at the grocery, with her thin red hair drawn severely back from her gaunt face, and a black shawl over her head. But as he looked up into her big, kind face, so full of Christmas sunshine, he wondered he could ever have thought her anything but lovely. The room was small and bare, but wonderfully gay with pine and bits of red and green crepe paper, saved from the 'fixins' at the store. And on a large bed in the corner sat the three little girls, Kitty with her bright curls bobbing, Josephine with her black braids sticking straight out, and the baby with tiny blue eyes that twinkled and shone like Harvey's.

The fine speech that Tom had been saying over to himself for the past two hours seemed to vanish into thin air before this excited little audience. But in faltering, stammering tones, which everyone was too excited to notice, he managed to say something about "Merry Christmas" and "good children" and then proceeded to open the magic sack. "Miss Kitty McGinnis!" he called, in deep, gruff tones. Kitty took the box he offered with shy embarrassment, slowly drew back the lid and gave a cry of amazement and delight. "A doll, O the loveliest doll that ever was!" she cried. Then turning to her brother, she whispered as softly as excitement would permit, "O Harvey, I'm afeard ye paid too much!"

"Aw, go on!" said Harvey, his face more like a full moon than ever. "Don't ye know that Santy kin do whatever he wants to?"

The other dolls were received with raptures, Josephine stroking the golden curls of the Lady Matilda with wondering fingers, and the baby dancing round and round, waving the pink-robed Lady Clarabel above her head.

"Mr. Harvey McGinnis!" came the gruff tones of Santa Claus; and Harvey smiled over to his mother as he drew out a pair of stout cloth gloves.

"Mrs. McGinnis!" And that good lady smiled back, as she shook out a dainty white apron with a coarse embroidery ruffle.

"I reckon Santy wanted you to wear that of a Sunday afternoon," said Harvey, awkwardly.

"And I'll be proud to do it!" said his mother.

Little sacks of candy were next produced and everyone settled down to enjoy it, thinking that the bottom of the big sack must be reached, when Santa called out in tones that trembled beneath the gruffness, "Another package for Mr. Harvey McGinnis!"

"Fer me—why—what—" said Harvey, taking the heavy oblong bundle; then, as the sparkling "Club House" skates met his view, his face lit up with a glory that Tom never forgot. The glory lasted but a moment, then he turned a troubled face toward the bulky old saint.

"You never ought to a done it," he said. "These must have cost a lot!"

"Aw, go on," was the reply in a distinctly boyish tone, "don't you know that Santy can do whatever he wants to?" and, with a prodigious bow, old Santa was gone.

A few minutes later, a slender boy with a bundle under his arm, was skating swiftly down the shining river in the moonlight. As he rounded the bend, a tall figure in a fur-trimmed coat came skimming slowly toward him, and a voice called out in Ralph Evans' condescending tones, "Well, how are the 'Jolly Ramblers' doing tonight?"

But the answer, this time, was clear and glad and triumphant. "The best in the world," said Tom, "and isn't this the glorious night for skating?"

THE WORKER IN SANDALWOOD*

By Marjorie L. C. Pickthall

The good curé of Terminaison says that this tale of Hyacinthe's is all a dream. But then Madame points triumphantly to the little cabinet of sandalwood in the corner of her room. It had stood there for many years now, and the dust has gathered in the fine lines of the little birds' feathers, and softened the petals of the lilies carved at the corners. And the wood has taken on a golden gleam like the memory of a sunset.

"What of that, my friend?" says Madame, pointing to the cabinet. And the old curé bows his head.

"It may be so. God is very good," he says gently. But he is never quite sure what he may believe.

On that winter day long ago, Hyacinthe was quite sure of one thing and that was that the workshop was very cold. There was no fire in it, and only one little lamp when the early dark drew on. The tools were so cold they scorched his fingers, and feet were so cold he danced clumsily in the shavings to warm them. He was a great clumsy boy of fourteen, dark-faced, dull-eyed, and uncared for. He was clumsy because it is impossible to be graceful when you are growing very fast and have not enough to eat. He was dull-eyed because all eyes met his unlovingly. He was uncared for because no one knew the beauty of his soul. But his heavy young hands could carve things like birds and flowers perfectly. On this winter evening he was just wondering if he might lay aside the

119

tools, and creep home to the cold loft where he slept, when he heard Pierre L'Oreillard's voice shouting outside.

"Be quick, be quick, and open the door, thou *imbecile*. It is I, thy master."

"*Oui, mon maître,*" said Hyacinthe, and he shambled to the door and opened it.

"Slow worm!" cried Pierre, and he cuffed Hyacinthe as he passed in. Hyacinthe rubbed his head and said nothing. He was used to blows. He wondered why his master was in the workshop at that time of day instead of drinking brandy at the Cinq Chateaux.

Pierre L'Oreillard had a small heavy bundle under his arm, wrapped in sacking, and then in burlap, and then in fine soft cloths. He laid it on a pile of shavings, and unfolded it carefully; and a dim sweetness filled the dark shed and hung heavily in the thin winter sunbeams.

"It is a piece of wood," said Hyacinthe in slow surprise. He knew that such wood had never been seen in Terminaison.

Pierre L'Oreillard rubbed the wood respectfully with his knobby fingers.

"It is sandalwood," he explained to Hyacinthe, pride of knowledge making him quite amiable, "a most precious wood that grows in warm countries, thou great goblin. Smell it, idiot. It is sweeter than cedar. It is to make a cabinet for the old Madame at the big house."

"*Oui, mon maître*," said the dull Hyacinthe.

"Thy great hands shall shape and smooth the wood, *nigaud*, and I will render it beautiful," said Pierre, puffing out his chest.

"Yes, Master," answered Hyacinthe humbly, "and when is it to be ready for Madame?"

"Madame will want it perhaps next week, for that is Christmas. It is to be finished and ready on the holy festival, great sluggard. Hearest thou?" and he cuffed Hyacinthe's ears again furiously.

Hyacinthe knew that the making of the cabinet would fall to him, as most of the other work did. When Pierre L'Oreillard was gone he touched the strange sweet wood and at last laid his cheek against it, while the fragrance caught his breath. "How it is beautiful!" said Hyacinthe, and for a moment his eyes glowed, and he was happy. Then the light passed and with bent head he shuffled back to his bench through a foam of white shavings curling almost to his knees.

"Madame will want the cabinet for Christmas," repeated Hyacinthe to himself, and fell to work harder than ever, though it was so cold in the shed that his breath hung in the air like a little silvery cloud. There was a tiny window on his right, through which, when it was clear of frost, one looked on Terminaison; and that was cheerful, and made him whistle. But to the left, through the chink of the ill-fitting door, there was nothing to be seen but the forest, and the road dying under the snow.

Brandy was good at the Cinq Chateaux and Pierre L'Oreillard gave Hyacinthe plenty of directions, but no further help with the cabinet.

"That is to be finished for Madame at the festival, sluggard," said he every day, cuffing Hyacinthe about the head, "finished, and with a prettiness about the corners, hearest thou, *ourson*?"

"Yes, Monsieur," said Hyacinthe in his slow way; "I will try to finish it. But if I hurry I shall spoil it."

Pierre's little eyes flickered. "See that it is done, and done properly. I suffer from a delicacy of the constitution and a little feebleness of the legs these days, so that I cannot handle the tools properly. I must leave this work to thee, *gacheur*. And stand up and touch a hand to thy cap when I speak to thee, slow-worm."

"Yes, monsieur," said Hyacinthe wearily.

It is hard to do all the work and to be beaten into the bargain. And fourteen is not very old. Hyacinthe worked on at the cabinet with his slow and exquisite skill. But on Christmas eve he was still at work, and the cabinet unfinished.

"The master will beat me," thought Hyacinthe, and he trembled a little, for Pierre's beatings were cruel. "But if I hurry, I shall spoil the wood, and it is too beautiful to be spoiled."

But he trembled again when Pierre came into the workshop, and he stood up and touched his cap.

"Is the cabinet finished, *imbecile*?" asked Pierre. And Hyacinthe answered in a low voice, "No, it is not finished yet, monsieur."

"Then work on it all night, and show it to me completed in the morning, or thy bones shall mourn thine idleness," said Pierre, with a wicked look in his little eyes. And he shut Hyacinthe into the shed with a smoky lamp, his tools, and the sandalwood cabinet.

It was nothing unusual. He had been often left before to finish a piece of work overnight while Pierre went off to his brandies. But this was Christmas eve, and he was very tired. Even the scent of the sandalwood could not make him fancy he was warm. The world seemed to be a black place, full of suffering and despair.

"In all the world, I have no friend," said Hyacinthe, staring at the flame of the lamp. "In all the world, there is no one to care whether I live or die. In all the world, no place, no heart, no love. O kind God, is there a place, a love for me in another world?"

I hope you feel very sorry for Hyacinthe, lonely, and cold, and shut up in the workshop on the eve of Christmas. He was but an overgrown, unhappy child. And I think with old Madame that for unhappy children, at this season, no help seems too divine for faith.

"There is no one to care for me," said Hyacinthe. And he even looked at the chisel in his hand, thinking that by a touch of that he might lose it all, and be at peace, somewhere, not far from God. Only it was forbidden. Then came the tears, and great sobs that shook him, so that he scarcely heard the gentle rattling of the latch.

He stumbled to the door, opening it on the still woods and the frosty stars. And a lad who stood outside in the snow said, "I see you are working late, comrade. May I come in?"

Hyacinthe brushed his ragged sleeve across his eyes and nodded "Yes." Those little villages strung along the great river see strange wayfarers at times. And Hyacinthe said to himself that surely here was such a one. Blinking into the stranger's eyes, he lost for a flash the first impression of youth, and received one of incredible age or sadness. But the wanderer's eyes were only quiet, very quiet, like the little pools in the wood where the wild does went to drink. As he turned within the door, smiling at Hyacinthe and shaking some snow from his cap, he did not seem to be more than sixteen or so.

"It is very cold outside," he said. "There is a big oak tree on the edge of the fields that had split in the frost and frightened all the little squirrels asleep there. Next year it will make an even better home for them. And see what I found close by!" He opened his fingers and showed Hyacinthe a little sparrow lying unruffled in the palm.

"*Pauvrette!*" said the dull Hyacinthe. "*Pauvrette!* Is it then dead?" He touched it with a gentle forefinger.

"No," answered the strange boy, "it is not dead. We will put it here among the shavings, not far from the lamp, and it will be well by the morning."

He smiled at Hyacinthe again, and the shambling lad felt dimly as if the scent of the sandalwood were sweeter, and the lamp-flame clearer. But the stranger's eyes were only quiet, quiet.

"Have you come far?" asked Hyacinthe. "It is a bad season for traveling, and the wolves are out."

"A long way," said the other. "A long, long way. I heard a child cry—"

"There is no child here," put in Hyacinthe. "Monsieur L'Oreillard says children cost too much money. But if you have come far, you must need food and fire, and I have neither. At the Cinq Chateaux you will find both."

The stranger looked at him again with those quiet eyes, and Hyacinthe fancied that his face was familiar. "I will stay here," he said; "you are late at work, and you are unhappy."

"Why as to that," answered Hyacinthe, rubbing his cheeks and ashamed of his tears, "most of are sad at one time or another, the good God knows. Stay here and welcome if it pleases you; and you may take a share of my bed, though it is no more than a pile of balsam boughs and an old blanket in the loft. But I must work at this cabinet, for the drawers must be finished and the handles put on and the corners carved, all by the holy morning; or my wages will be paid with a stick."

"You have a hard master," put in the other, "if he would pay you with blows upon the feast of Noel."

"He is hard enough," said Hyacinthe, "but once he gave me a dinner of sausages and white wine; and once, in the summer, melons. If my eyes will stay open, I will finish this by morning. Stay with me an hour or so, comrade, and talk to me of your travels, so that the time may pass more quickly."

And while Hyacinthe worked, he told,—of sunshine and dust, of the shadow of vine-leaves on the flat white walls of a house; of rosy doves on the roof; of the flowers that come out in the spring, anemones crimson and blue, and white cyclamen in the shadow of the rocks; of the olive, the myrtle, and the almond; until Hyacinthe's fingers ceased working, and his sleepy eyes blinked wonderingly.

"See what you have done, comrade," he said at last; "you have told me of such pretty things that I have done but little work for an hour. And now the cabinet will never be finished, and I shall be beaten."

"Let me help you," smiled the other. "I also was bred a carpenter."

At first Hyacinthe would not, fearing to trust the sweet wood out of his own hands. But at length he allowed the stranger to fit in one of the drawers. And so deftly was it done that Hyacinthe pounded his fists on the bench in admiration. "You have a pretty knack," he cried. "It seemed as if you did but hold the drawer in your hands a moment, and hey! it jumped into its place."

"Let me fit in the other little drawers while you rest awhile," said the stranger. So Hyacinthe curled up among the shavings, and the other boy fell to work upon the little cabinet of sandalwood.

Hyacinthe was very tired. He lay still among the shavings, and thought of all the boy had told him, of the hillside flowers, the laughing leaves, the golden bloom of the anise, and the golden sun upon the roads until he was warm. And all the time the boy with the quiet eyes was at work upon the cabinet, smoothing, fitting, polishing.

"You do better work than I," said Hyacinthe once, and the stranger answered, "I was lovingly taught." And again Hyacinthe said, "It is growing towards morning. In a little while I will get up and help you."

"Lie still and rest," said the other boy. And Hyacinthe lay still. His thoughts began to slide into dreams, and he woke with a little start, for there seemed to be music in the shed; though he could not tell whether it came from the strange boy's lips, or from the shappy tools as he used them, or from the stars.

"The stars are much paler," thought Hyacinthe. "Soon it will be morning, and the corners are not carved yet. I must get up and help this kind one in a little moment. Only the music and the sweetness seem to fold me close, so that I may not move."

Then behind the forest there shone a pale glow of dawn, and in Terminaison the church bells began to ring. "Day will soon be here," thought Hyacinthe, "and with day will come Monsieur L'Oreillard and his stick. I must get up and help for even yet the corners are not carved."

But the stranger looked at him, smiling as though he loved him, and laid his brown finger lightly on the four empty corners of the cabinet. And Hyacinthe saw the squares of reddish wood ripple and heave and break, as little clouds when the wind goes through the sky. And out of them thrust forth the little birds, and after them the lilies, for a moment living; but even as Hyacinthe looked, settling back into the sweet reddish-brown wood. Then the stranger smiled again, laid all the tools in order, and, opening the door, went away into the woods.

Hyacinthe crept slowly to the door. The winter sun, half risen, filled all the frosty air with splendid gold. Far down the road a figure seemed to move amid the glory, but the splendor was such that Hyacinthe was blinded. His breath came sharply as the glow beat on the wretched shed, on the old shavings, on the cabinet with the little birds and the lilies carved at the corners.

He was too pure of heart to feel afraid. But "Blessed be the Lord," whispered Hyacinthe, clasping his slow hands, "for He hath visited and redeemed His people. But who will believe?"

Then the sun of Christ's day rose gloriously, and the little sparrow came from his nest among the shavings and shook his wings to the light.

*Reprinted by permission of the publishers of "Everyland."

THE SHEPHERD WHO DIDN'T GO*

By Jay T. Stocking

You have all heard of the shepherds who went to Bethlehem, but I do not believe any of you have heard of the shepherd who didn't go. The Bible does not say anything about him, but his story has come to me, and I am going to tell it to you.

The city of Bethlehem stood on a hill. Below the town, with its steep narrow streets and white walls, were gray olive orchards. Below the orchards were gardens bright with flowers. Below the gardens lay green meadows, and beyond these pasture-lands that stretched away to the wilderness plains where little patches of grass grew among the bushes and between the great rocks. There were caves among these rocks where wolves used to skulk and sometimes robbers hid. So the shepherds who guarded their flocks in these wild pastures dared not leave them alone.

One clear beautiful night, many centuries ago, four shepherds were watching their flocks on these pastures. Samuel, Ezra, Joel, and Dahvid were their names. Samuel, Ezra, and Joel were strong men, no longer young, with shaggy eyebrows and brown beards; Ezra's was short, Joel's long, and Samuel's streaked with gray. They owned the flocks which they tended. Dahvid was a boy with ruddy cheeks, bright eyes, and strong lithe limbs. He cared for the flocks of old Abraham. Abraham was old and rich, and did not work any more, but hired Dahvid, whose family was very poor, to care for his sheep.

The flocks of the four shepherds were lying quiet on the plain far below the city, and near by Samuel, Ezra, Joel, and Dahvid lay wrapped in their shepherds' cloaks.

"Samuel," said Dahvid, rising upon his elbow.

"What is it, Dahvid?" asked the other in a deep voice.

"Are you not glad that you tend sheep in Bethlehem instead of some distant place?"

"Why, Dahvid?" asked Samuel sleepily.

"Because it is in Bethlehem that the King we have been looking for so long is to be born. I have been reading it in the prophets only today."

"Have you only just heard of that?" asked Ezra sourly.

"No," replied the boy hotly. "I have heard my mother tell of it ever since I can remember, and I have read it over and over again. Samuel!"

"Yes, Dahvid?"

"Do you think we shall ever see the promised King?"

"I do not know, my boy," the older man answered sadly. "We have waited long, and there seems little hope for Israel now. But he will come some day, he will come some day. Why do you ask, Dahvid?"

"I cannot tell. It is often in my mind. Something makes me think of it tonight. Perhaps it is because I read of him today. Samuel, I would walk to the end of the earth to see the Christ-child."

"Well, you need not start now," grumbled Ezra, and Joel added roughly, "Go to sleep, boy, the hour is late."

It was much later before Dahvid fell asleep, for his head was full of dreams, and the stories of wonderful days to come that his mother had told him. But at length he joined the rest in healthy slumber.

Suddenly it seemed to each of them that something had passed over him, and touched him lightly on the cheek. The older men raised themselves on their elbows, but Dahvid sprang to his feet. At first they saw only a great light, which nearly blinded them, then they discerned a shining form in the sky, and heard a voice saying: "Be not afraid; for behold, I bring you good tidings of great joy which shall be to all the people; for there is born to you this day in the city of David a Saviour, who is Christ the Lord. And this is the sign unto you: Ye shall find a babe wrapped in swaddling clothes and lying in a manger."

And then all the sky was full of light, and the air was full of heavenly voices, singing, "Glory to God in the highest, and on earth peace, good will toward men."

While the shepherds listened, half joyful, half afraid, the light faded and the voices floated away—"Good will to men—to men—to men," and all was still as before. For a moment the shepherds looked at each other in silent awe and wonder. Then Ezra spoke in a voice dry with fear. "What was it?"

Dahvid stood speechless, and Samuel answered reverently, "Angels."

"Brothers," he continued, "a wonderful thing has happened to us. It has been a long, long day since angels have spoken to men."

Then he girded his shepherd's cloak about him and seized his staff. "Come, Ezra, Joel, Dahvid, let us be going."

"Going—where?" asked Ezra and Joel.

"Why, to Bethlehem to see the Child. Did not the angel tell us the sign? Let us go at once to find the babe wrapped in swaddling clothes and lying in a manger."

"There be many mangers in Bethlehem," objected Ezra.

"I know not how we shall find him," said Joel. "It is a vain search, I fear," and he drew his cloak about him and reached for his staff, "but I will go with you if you say."

So they started, Samuel, Ezra, and Joel—but Dahvid stood still.

"Come, Dahvid, make haste!" called Samuel.

But the boy did not move.

"I cannot go," he said.

"Cannot go!" cried Samuel in amazement; and Ezra added, "Who said but a little while ago that he would go to the end of the earth to see the King?"

"And so I would," cried Dahvid; "but the sheep—we cannot leave the sheep alone."

"The sheep will be safe enough," said Samuel. "The dogs will keep them together. There are no wolves tonight. Come, Dahvid."

But the boy was firm. "There is my master; he'll be angry if I leave his flocks alone."

"Old Abraham will never know," said Joel.

"Abraham is a hard master," said Dahvid. "Many a time I have felt his heavy staff on my back. But it is not that which keeps me. I have given him my word that, come day, come night, come life, come death, I will not fail to keep the flocks. Go on without me; I must keep my word. Go on."

So they went on, impatient and eager for this wondrous quest, Ezra and Joel muttering now and then at the obstinacy of the boy, but Samuel full of glowing admiration. Dahvid watched them as they moved up the hill. That dream of finding the Christ-child— how could he give it up? Once he started forward: "I will go!" But something held him back, and he threw himself on the ground and kept back tears of bitter disappointment. After a time he grew calmer, and found a certain comfort in thinking of the helplessness of his flock.

Suddenly the low growling of his dog brought him to his feet. But he saw nothing, heard nothing, and bade the dog be still. In a moment, with a bark of alarm, the dog was up again and away. Dahvid sprang up, certain now that danger was near. There was panic in the flock. Toward the wilderness he could see lean, gray forms, moving stealthily and swiftly among the sheep. Wolves! Springing upon a rock, and waving his cloak in circles about his head, he uttered the familiar call which gathered the sheep about him, his own sheep nearest, and behind them the flocks of Samuel, Ezra, and Joel. The wolves made off and Dahvid quickly looked over his flock to see if all were there—for the Eastern shepherd knows his sheep by name.

One by one he named them, with an increasing feeling of relief. They were all there. No! One was missing—Ke-barbara, the pet of the flock. Ke-barbara means striped, and the little sheep was so called because of the dark marking of her fleece. After waving his staff over the huddled beasts, and uttering a few times the soothing cry, "Hoo-o-o, ta-a-a! hoo-o-o, ta-a-a!" he rushed off in the direction which the wolves had taken. At the top of the steep bank, at the edge of the pasture, he stopped and called, "Ke-barbara! Ke-barbara!" and for answer heard an anguished bleat from the rocks below.

It was a steep and slippery way, but Dahvid plunged down with no thought of anything but the sheep. Loose stones gave way and he lost his footing. At the bottom he picked himself up unhurt, and there beside him were two wolves quarreling over the wounded sheep. One of them slunk away at sight of the boy, but the other had a taste of blood and sprang at Dahvid, missing his throat but sinking his teeth into his leg. Then Dahvid, as the beast turned to spring again, struck him a heavy blow on the head with his staff and killed him. His own wounds were bleeding and painful, but he turned at once with caressing words to the sheep.

"Ke-barbara, they have hurt you, little sheep! But they have not killed you! I reached you just in time. You cannot walk; can you? And I am afraid I cannot carry you. But I can help. There, put your head on my arm." He groaned with pain. "No, the other one." So he talked to her, as to a child, as the wounded boy and the wounded sheep slowly made their way up the steep hillside and over the rough rocks. It was not a long way, and, half an hour before, the sturdy shepherd lad would have bounded over it quickly enough. But now the wounded leg was slow, the wounded arm was weak, and the wounded lamb seemed very heavy. It was a weary journey, with many stops. When at last they reached the flock, still huddled trembling together, Dahvid had only strength to give one reassuring "Hoo-o-o, ta-a-a," then fell exhausted.

How long he lay there he did not know, but the dawn was growing bright when three men appeared from the direction of the town. It was not the shepherds, but old Abraham and two of his servants. As the old man caught sight of his flock, but he saw no shepherd, he raged with anger. "Dahvid!" he shouted fiercely. "Dahvid!" There was no answer.

"The young vagabond! He has left the sheep. Of great worth are his promises! He would keep my flock. 'Come life—come death!' Dahvid! Let me once find him and I will give him something he will remember longer than he does his vows."

As he drew near the flock he discovered the boy lying on the ground. "Ah, asleep is he? and the sun this high! Come, get up!" he shouted fiercely, and lifted his staff to strike. But, as he did so he caught sight of the white face and the bleeding arm, and noticed the wounded sheep. Old Abraham dropped his angry arm, and there was a touch of tenderness that was strange to him, as he continued: "Ah, Dahvid, boy! You did not forget your promises; did you, Dahvid? And I would have struck you! Forgive me, my lad." Then, turning to his servants, he gave them command: "Take him to the inn and bid them care for him. I, myself, will keep the flock today."

The servants bowed low, "The inn is full, my lord."

Old Abraham commanded again positively, "Take him to the inn, I say."

"But the inn is full, my lord," replied the older servant, trembling.

Then the other servant spoke, "There is perhaps room in the stable, my lord."

"Then bear him thither, and bid them give him the best of care. Go at once."

So the servants bore Dahvid away, still unconscious from his wounds and made him comfortable on a bed of straw in the stable of the inn.

It was some hours before he came to himself. When at last he opened his eyes, and his ears began to catch once more the sounds about him, the first thing he heard was a faint cry.

"What is that?" he asked eagerly of Samuel, who was watching beside him.

"That," said the old shepherd, in tones of mingled joy and reverence, "is the Child the angels told us about, the Child we came to see. We found him here in the stable, in a manger."

"And I am not to see him?"

"Yes, you are," said Samuel, and a grave-faced man brought the Child and laid Him in Dahvid's arms, the Child for whose coming the people had been longing for a thousand years.

The color at length came back to Dahvid's white cheeks and strength and health to his limbs and he went back again to the plain. Old Abraham embraced him, "Forgive me, my son. I have been a hard master. Thou hast been very faithful, and for thy reward I make thee lord over all my flocks and half of them shall be thine own."

So Dahvid became a man of flocks, and all his days he was known among the other shepherds as the one who had held the Christ-child in his arms. And there was none among them who was thought so brave, and gentle, and wise as the *Shepherd Who Didn't Go*.

*Reprinted by permission from "The City that Never Was Reached," by Jay T. Stocking; published by the Pilgrim Press.

PAULINA'S CHRISTMAS*

A Story of Russian Life. Adapted from Anna Robinson's *Little Paulina*

One day, in Russia, there was a heavy snowstorm. The snow was deep on the ground; and in the forest the branches of the trees bent under its weight.

In this forest a little girl was struggling along. There was no path for her to follow, for the snow covered all the paths. The little girl's name was Paulina. She was dressed in a long fur coat, and she wore a cap and mittens and gaiters of fur, so that she looked more like a little furry animal than a little girl. She kept tramping along, not a bit afraid, when suddenly she heard a call for help.

"Help! Help!" the call came.

"Coming, coming!" she called back. She went in the direction of the voice and soon she saw a man making his way toward her. His dress was that of a peasant.

"Will you please direct me out of this forest, little one?" he asked. "You probably know the paths about."

"No, I am a stranger here," Paulina answered. "I live in Kief—that is, I did live there; but I am on my way to my father."

"Where is your father?" asked the man.

"He is in Siberia. They banished him."

"But, little one," said the stranger, "that is a terrible place for a child to go to. That frozen country, where wicked people are sent!"

"O, yes,—but my father is there, you know," said Paulina.

"Who is your father?" the man asked.

The little girl was about to tell him, when she noticed a look of interest on the stranger's face, so she said,

"Did you say that you had lost your way in the forest? Do you live far from here?"

"Yes, very far. I am lost, and am nearly perishing from hunger and cold. How far is it to the next village?"

"They told me it was some miles on," said the child. "But I will take you back to the woodsman's cottage where I spent the night. The woman is a kind-hearted person, and I am sure she will give you shelter."

"That is kind of you, little one," said the stranger, "but you will be hindering your own journey if you do that."

"I know that my father would want me to show a kindness, even though it did put me back some," Paulina said.

"You must have a good father, to give you such training. Why did the Emperor send him into exile?" the stranger asked her.

"O, my father had enemies who lied to the Emperor—and there was no chance given to my father to explain. So the Emperor sent him away to Siberia,—and I am trying to find my way there to him."

While they walked through the forest, the stranger told Paulina about his own little daughter who was expecting him to spend Christmas with her. At last they reached the woodsman's hut. The woman greeted them kindly, and while Paulina went into another room to help her prepare the evening meal, the stranger was left warming himself by the fire, and rocking the cradle.

Once Paulina thought she heard voices, as if the stranger were talking to someone; but when she went back, she found him alone, still warming his hands and rocking the cradle with his foot.

That night the stranger slept on the floor in front of the fire—there was no other place for him; but he was glad to be safe from the storm outside.

Early in the morning, the two started out through the forest again. They must hurry, if they were to reach the next village before darkness fell. The storm had passed over, and the day was cold and clear. A beautiful winter's day. The little girl and the stranger reached the village on the other side of the forest early in the afternoon, and there before them they saw a beautiful sleigh drawn by four horses. There were four servants standing near.

"What a lovely sleigh!" exclaimed Paulina.

"Yes, I wonder where they are going. I will ask them," the stranger said. He went nearer the men and spoke to them.

"We are driving for our master to Igorhof," they said.

"Why, that is where my daughter is. If I might only ride with you, I could spend Christmas with her. Tomorrow is Christmas day, you know. And, little one, you could spend Christmas with us, too.'

"O, no," said Paulina. "I could not take the time. I must hurry on to my father. But it would be lovely if we could only ride in this beautiful sleigh."

"You could spend the night with us, and then we could set you on your way, because you have been so kind to me," the man told her.

The servants were willing to let them ride in the beautiful sleigh, and soon they were speeding over the snow toward the great city. Once, the stranger took a scarf from a pocket on the side of the sleigh and threw it about his neck. Paulina frowned, and promptly placed it back in the pocket.

"It isn't right for you to touch anything in the sleigh. It belongs to someone else. I am beginning to fear that you may not be an honest man," she said gravely.

The stranger laughed at her, but he did not take the scarf again. They sped on over the snow until, as darkness fell, they reached the city. Soon they entered a large courtyard, and the stranger took Paulina's hand and led her into a narrow passageway, and up a small winding stairway.

"Where are you taking me?" asked Paulina. "I feel almost sure now, that you are not an honest man. I think that you may even be a thief!"

The man laughed again.

"No, I am an honest man. You will believe me when you see my little daughter. I trusted you in the forest. Now you trust me."

He led her into a large room, and they sat down upon a sofa.

"We will wait here until my daughter comes," he said.

Soon the door opened, and a beautiful little girl, about as large as Paulina, came toward them. She looked puzzled when she saw the rough-looking man with the little girl. She went close to the stranger and looked into his face.

"It is my father!" she cried, and threw her arms around his neck.

"But why are you dressed like a peasant? Has there been an accident? And who is this little stranger?"

The man took her on his lap and told her how his sleigh had been overturned in the storm, and how he had found his way to a peasant's hut, where they had given him dry clothes to put on, and how he had started out alone to find his way through the forest; and how he was nearly perishing with cold and hunger when this little girl had rescued him, and how, if it had not been for her, he would have died in the snow in the forest. He told her how little Paulina was on her way to Siberia to find her father, and how they went to the woodsman's hut where a servant had found him, and how he had planned for the sleigh to meet them on the other side of the forest.

"O," Paulina interrupted him, "then there was somebody talking with you when we were preparing the evening meal?"

"Yes, and everything came out just as I had planned. And do you know, little daughter, this Paulina would not let me put my own scarf around my neck. She thought that I was a thief. She is an honest little girl. But she will not tell me her name. She does not trust me."

"But why should I trust you, when you will not tell me who you are, or anything about yourself?" Paulina asked.

"Do trust my father, Paulina. I'm sure he can help you. He will tell you who he is soon, I know," the beautiful little girl said.

"Yes, little one," the stranger said. "I know someone who could speak to the Emperor about your father, and perhaps he could be pardoned. Please tell me your name; and then before you go away I will answer any questions about myself you may ask me."

"Do tell my father, Paulina," the little girl urged.

Paulina threw her arms about the stranger's knees.

"O, if you could only get the Emperor to pardon him.—But I do not ask for a *pardon*—he has done nothing to be pardoned for. All that I ask is that he may have justice done him. My father is Vladimir Betzkoi."

The stranger frowned, and then he whispered,

"There must be some mistake. He must be a good man to have such an honest little daughter." Then he said to Paulina,

"Do you believe now that I am an honest man, since you have seen my daughter?"

"O, yes, indeed I do. You couldn't help being good and honest. She is so beautiful. I think her face is like what a queen's should be," Paulina answered eagerly.

The stranger and his little daughter smiled, and the man said,

"Well, I believe that your father is an honest man since I have seen you. And I can tell you now, I know he will be pardoned."

"Tell her, father, tell the little Paulina who you are," his daughter whispered.

"Until your father returns to you, little one, you must stay here and I will be a father to you—as I am father to all the people of Russia, for I am the Emperor!"

Just then the bells began ringing, and voices outside began singing,—for it was the beginning of Christmas morning. And Paulina said,

"This is the happiest Christmas morning I have ever known."

*By permission—Copyright, 1912, by Sturgis & Walton Company.

UNTO US A CHILD IS BORN

As Told by Phebe A. Curtiss at a "White Gift" Service

It was in the little town of Bethlehem, with its white walls and narrow streets, that a wonderful thing happened many, many years ago. The whole aspect of the place had been completely transformed, and instead of the quiet which usually existed there, confusion reigned. The little town was crowded full of people. All day long men, women and children had been pouring in companies into it until every available place was full. It had something to do with the payment of taxes, and the people had come from far and near in response to the call of those in authority.

Many of them were staying with relatives and friends, and every door had been opened to receive those who came. There were not many places where the public could go to stay in those days, and the ones that there were had been already filled.

Just as the shadows were closing down around the hill, an interesting little group found its way up the winding path through the orchards, touched as they were by the sunset coloring, and into the gate of the city. The man, seemingly about fifty years of age, walked with slow and measured tread. He had a black beard, lightly sprinkled with gray, and he carried in his hand a staff, which served him in walking and also in persuading the donkey he was leading to move a little more rapidly.

It was plain to see that the errand he had come on was an important one, both from the care with which he was dressed and from the anxious look which now and then spread over his face.

Upon the donkey's back sat a woman, and your attention would have been directed to her at once if you could have been there. She was marvelously beautiful. She was very young—just at that interesting period between girlhood and womanhood, when the charm is so great.

Her eyes were large and blue and they were a prominent feature in the face that was absolutely perfect in contour and coloring.

She wore an outer robe of a dull woolen stuff which covered the blue garment worn underneath—the garment which indicated that she was a virgin. Over her head and around her neck she wore the customary white veil or "wimple."

As the donkey jogged along, stopping now and then to nibble at the bushes on either side, she sat calmly looking out upon the surroundings. Once in a while she would draw aside her veil and her beautiful eyes would lift themselves to heaven with a look of rapture and adoration in them, which was wonderful to see.

As they drew nearer to the town the look of anxiety upon the face of the man deepened, for he began to realize more and more the crowded condition of the place they were approaching. The hurry and bustle and confusion made themselves felt far beyond the bounds of the town itself.

They seemed to be strangers—at least they did not have relatives or friends to whom they could turn; and the man started at once to make his way to the inn or "kahn," as it was called in those days.

This inn was a quadrangular building made of rough stones. It was one story high, with a flat roof, and it had not a single window. All around it was a high wall, built of rocks; and the space between that wall and the building made a safe enclosure for the animals.

The thing about these inns that would surprise you or me today was the way in which the business connected with them was run. There was no charge made for staying there, but safe lodging was freely given. Each company which came brought its own bedding, its own food and everything they needed to use in cooking. A resting place and safe protection were all that were offered. The inn was in charge of one caretaker. There were no other servants.

As the traveler, whose name was Joseph, drew near he found to his dismay that he could not even make his way through the crowd to the gate keeper, who was guarding the one entrance to the inn.

He decided to leave Mary, his wife, in the company of a family with whom he had been talking while he made an effort to gain entrance.

When at last he reached the man in charge, he found it was just as he had feared. The inn was full—there was no room for them there.

In vain he urged; he told of his own line of ancestors; of the noble line from which his wife descended. The answer was always the same: "There is no room."

At last he pleaded for Mary, his wife. He told the man in charge that she was not strong, that she had come a long, long way and was very tired; and urged that some place be found for her. He feared the results if she should be compelled to stay in the open all night.

So earnestly he pleaded his case that at last the man said, "I have no room and yet I cannot turn you away; come with me and I will find you a place in the stable."

Joseph then found Mary and they and the ones with whom she had been tarrying went together to the stable and there made themselves comfortable for the night.

This was not at all the cross to them that it would seem to you today. It was a very common thing indeed for people to stay in the stables when the inn was full. And then, too, you must remember that they were descended from a long line of shepherds. They naturally loved the animals and did not feel at all badly to sleep where they had been, or even in very close company with them.

We can imagine that it was with very thankful hearts they lay down to rest that night.

There was a company of men, asleep in the pasture lands at some little distance from Bethlehem, on the slope of the hill. They were shepherds. They had cared for their sheep and after that all but one of them had lain down to sleep. It was their custom for all of the number to watch while the others slept. They were wrapped in their great, warm shepherd's cloaks, for the air was chilly at that season. All at once a strange thing happened. It began to grow very light, and the one who was watching could not understand. He spoke to the others and they sprang to their feet.

Brighter and brighter shone the light until it was like the day, and you can imagine that the shepherds were startled. They could not speak, so great was their astonishment; but as they drew closer together they heard a voice coming out of the light. The voice said, "Be not afraid. Behold, I bring you good tidings of great joy, which shall be to all people. For unto you is born this day, in the city of David, a Saviour which is Christ the Lord. And this shall be a sign unto you; ye shall find the babe wrapped in swaddling clothes lying in a manger."

And then there were with this angel, who spoke, many other angels; and they sang, praising God, saying, "Glory to God in the highest, and on earth peace, good will toward men."

They sang it again and again until the heavens fairly rang with it.

For a while after the beautiful song had died away and the light had failed, the shepherds stood with bowed heads. Then each one gathered his cloak around him and took his staff in his hand and they started together to find the place and the Child about which they had heard.

Hastening into Bethlehem they came to the inn and found Joseph and Mary, and the babe, lying in the manger, just as the angel said they would. They worshipped the Child and returned to their duties, praising God and glorifying Him.

After that Joseph and Mary went away to another place and took the child Jesus with them, and many others came to worship Him. Among them were three Wise Men who had come from separate places and all from a great distance.

They followed the star which was set in the heavens to guide them and they too found the One they sought.

As they came into the place where He was, each one bowed in worship and they laid before Him the gifts they had brought—gold, frankincense and myrrh.

What a wonderful story it is, and how our hearts swell with love as we think about it! It is fitting that tonight we should dwell upon it, for we, too, have come to worship our King. It is His birthday and we have come together to bring Him our gifts. We have brought "white gifts" because they are the expression of our pure, unselfish love.

The Wise Men brought gold, and we have brought our gifts of *substance*—money and food and clothing and things that will help to make others comfortable and happy.

The Wise Men brought frankincense, and we bring gifts of *service*; for each one of us desires to do some one thing all during the year that will make for good and make us worthy followers of Him.

The Wise Men brought myrrh, and we bring devotion; for we bring the gift of *self.* If we have not already given ourselves to the Master, we want to do so now; and if we have done so, we want to reconsecrate our lives to Him.

THE STAR*

By Florence M. Kingsley

Once upon a time in a country far away from here, there lived a little girl named Ruth. Ruth's home was not at all like our houses, for she lived in a little tower on top of the great stone wall that surrounded the town of Bethlehem. Ruth's father was the hotel-keeper—the Bible says the "inn keeper." This inn was not at all like our hotels, either. There was a great open yard, which was called the courtyard. All about this yard were little rooms and each traveler who came to the hotel rented one. The inn stood near the great stone wall of the city, so that as Ruth stood, one night, looking out of the tower window, she looked directly into the courtyard. It was truly a strange sight that met her eyes. So many people were coming to the inn, for the King had made a law that every man should come back to the city where his father used to live to be counted and to pay his taxes. Some of the people came on the backs of camels, with great rolls of bedding and their dishes for cooking upon the back of the beast. Some of them came on little donkeys, and on their backs too were the bedding and the dishes. Some of the people came walking—slowly; they were so tired. Many miles some of them had come. As Ruth looked down into the courtyard, she saw the camels being led to their places by their masters, she heard the snap of the whips, she saw the sparks shoot up from the fires that were kindled in the courtyard, where each person was preparing his own supper; she heard the cries of the tired, hungry little children.

Presently her mother, who was cooking supper, came over to the window and said, "Ruthie, thou shalt hide in the house until all those people are gone. Dost thou understand?"

"Yes, my mother," said the child, and she left the window to follow her mother back to the stove, limping painfully, for little Ruth was a cripple. Her mother stooped suddenly and caught the child in her arms.

"My poor little lamb. It was a mule's kick, just six years ago, that hurt your poor back and made you lame."

"Never mind, my mother. My back does not ache today, and lately when the light of the strange new star has shone down upon my bed my back has felt so much stronger and I have felt so happy, as though I could climb upon the rays of the star and up, up into the sky and above the stars!"

Her mother shook her head sadly. "Thou art not likely to climb much, now or ever, but come, the supper is ready; let us go to find your father. I wonder what keeps him."

They found the father standing at the gate of the courtyard, talking to a man and woman who had just arrived. The man was tall, with a long beard, and he led by a rope a snow white mule, on which sat the drooping figure of the woman. As Ruth and her mother came near, they heard the father say, "But I tell thee that there is no more room in the inn. Hast thou no friends where thou canst go to spend the night?" The man shook his head. "No, none," he answered. "I care not for myself, but my poor wife." Little Ruth pulled at her mother's dress. "Mother, the oxen sleep out under the stars these warm nights and the straw in the caves is clean and warm; I have made a bed there for my little lamb."

Ruth's mother bowed before the tall man. "Thou didst hear the child. It is as she says—the straw is clean and warm." The tall man bowed his head. "We shall be very glad to stay," and he helped the sweet-faced woman down from the donkey's back and led her away to the cave stable, while the little Ruth and her mother hurried up the stairs that they might send a bowl of porridge to the sweet-faced woman, and a sup of new milk, as well.

That night when little Ruth lay down in her bed, the rays of the beautiful new star shone through the window more brightly than before. They seemed to soothe the tired aching shoulders. She fell asleep and dreamed that the beautiful, bright star burst and out of it came countless angels, who sang in the night:

"Glory to God in the highest, peace on earth, good will to men." And then it was morning and her mother was bending over her and saying, "Awake, awake, little Ruth. Mother has something to tell thee." Then as the eyes opened slowly—"The angels came in the night, little one, and left a Baby to lay beside your little white lamb in the manger."

That afternoon, Ruth went with her mother to the fountain. The mother turned aside to talk to the other women of the town about the strange things heard and seen the night before, but Ruth went on and sat down by the edge of the fountain. The child, was not frightened, for strangers came often to the well, but never had she seen men who looked like the three who now came towards her. The first one, a tall man with a long white beard, came close to Ruth and said, "Canst tell us, child, where is born he that is called the King of the Jews?"

"I know of no king," she answered, "but last night while the star was shining, the angels brought a baby to lie beside my white lamb in the manger." The stranger bowed his head. "That must be he. Wilt thou show us the way to Him, my child?" So Ruth ran and her mother led the three men to the cave and "when they saw the Child, they rejoiced with exceeding great joy, and opening their gifts, they presented unto Him gold, and frankincense and myrrh." with wonderful jewels, so that Ruth's mother's eyes shone with wonder, but little Ruth saw only the Baby, which lay asleep on its mother's breast.

"If only I might hold Him in my arms," she thought, but was afraid to ask.

After a few days, the strangers left Bethlehem, all but the three— the man, whose name was Joseph, and Mary, his wife, and the Baby. Then, as of old, little Ruth played about the courtyard and the white lamb frolicked at her side. Often she dropped to her knees to press the little woolly white head against her breast, while she murmured: "My little lamb, my very, very own. I love you, lambie," and then together they would steal over to the entrance of the cave to peep in at the Baby, and always she thought, "If I only might touch his hand," but was afraid to ask. One night as she lay in her bed, she thought to herself: "Oh, I wish I had a beautiful gift for him, such as the wise men brought, but I have nothing at all to offer and I love him so much." Just then the light of the star, which was nightly fading, fell across the foot of the bed and shone full upon the white lamb which lay asleep at her feet—and then she thought of something. The next morning she arose with her face shining with joy. She dressed carefully and with the white lamb held close to her breast, went slowly and painfully down the stairway and over to the door of the cave. "I have come," she said, "to worship Him, and I have brought Him—my white lamb." The mother smiled at the lame child, then she lifted the Baby from her breast and placed Him in the arms of the little maid who knelt at her feet.

A few days after, an angel came to the father, Joseph, and told him to take the Baby and hurry to the land of Egypt, for the wicked King wanted to do it harm, and so these three—the father, mother and Baby—went by night to the far country of Egypt. And the star grew dimmer and dimmer and passed away forever from the skies over Bethlehem, but little Ruth grew straight and strong and beautiful as the almond trees in the orchard, and all the people who saw her were amazed, for Ruth was once a cripple.

"It was the light of the strange star," her mother said, but little Ruth knew it was the touch of the blessed Christ-Child, who was once folded against her heart.

*Used by permission of the author and the publishers, Henry Altemus Company.

The End

www.ingramcontent.com/pod-product-compliance
Lightning Source LLC
Chambersburg PA
CBHW070656290526
45790CB00001B/338